Walter Coote

The Western Pacific

Being a Description of the Groups of Islands to the North and East of the Australian

Continent

Walter Coote

The Western Pacific
Being a Description of the Groups of Islands to the North and East of the Australian Continent

ISBN/EAN: 9783744730464

Printed in Europe, USA, Canada, Australia, Japan

Cover: Foto ©Andreas Hilbeck / pixelio.de

More available books at **www.hansebooks.com**

BEING

DESCRIPTION OF THE GROUPS OF ISLANDS TO THE NORTH AND EAST OF THE AUSTRALIAN CONTINENT.

BY

WALTER COOTE, F.R.G.S.,

AUTHOR OF "WANDERINGS SOUTH AND EAST," "THREE MONTHS IN THE MEDITERRANEAN," ETC.

WITH A MAP AND TWENTY-THREE ILLUSTRATIONS

Executed by E. WHYMPER *from Drawings by the Author.*

LONDON:
AMPSON LOW, MARSTON, SEARLE, AND RIVINGTON,
CROWN BUILDINGS, 188, FLEET STREET, E.C.
1883.

LONDON :
PRINTED BY WILLIAM CLOWES AND SONS, LIMITED,
STAMFORD STREET AND CHARING CROSS.

PREFACE.

THE attitude taken by the Australian Colonies with reference to the island-continent of New Guinea and the groups of islands in the Western Pacific, has taken England altogether by surprise. I venture also to think that the vast majority of English people find themselves entirely in the dark as regards the islands which it is proposed to annex. The present volume aims at giving some general idea of these islands from my own personal experience, and is mainly a reprint from a portion of a larger book of travel. The interest that has been so suddenly developed regarding this part of the globe has tempted me to add a few pages upon the subject of colonial extension in the Pacific, and I am hopeful that these, taken together with the accounts given of the various groups of islands, and the practices and abuses connected with the Labour Traffic, will enable my readers to form a clear and accurate opinion upon a series of questions, which—if we may judge from the attitude of the Australian public, and the gradually awakening interest shown by political and philanthropic parties in England—bid fair to become of considerable importance at home as well as in Australia.

WALTER COOTE.

LONDON, *September*, 1883.

CONTENTS.

	PAGE
INTRODUCTION	ix

CHAPTER I.
NORFOLK ISLAND 1

CHAPTER II.
FIJI—OVALAU AND MBAU 17

CHAPTER III.
FIJI—THE REWA DISTRICT . . . 35

CHAPTER IV.
THE NEW HEBRIDES 48

CHAPTER V.
THE NEW HEBRIDES—MAEWO . . . 59

CHAPTER VI.
THE BANKS AND TORRES ISLANDS . . . 72

CHAPTER VII.
THE SANTA CRUZ ISLANDS 85

CHAPTER VIII.
Santa Cruz—The Main Island . . . 102

CHAPTER IX.
The Solomon Islands — Ulaua and San Christoval 117

CHAPTER X.
The Solomon Islands—Malanta and Florida . 128

CHAPTER XI.
The Solomon Islands—Ysabel . . . 140

CHAPTER XII.
The Loyalty Islands 152

CHAPTER XIII.
New Caledonia 160

CHAPTER XIV.
Labour and Trade in the Western Pacific . 167

LIST OF ILLUSTRATIONS.

	PAGE
"The Town," Norfolk Island	6
Fiji Houses	38
A New Hebrides Village	61
Interior of the Hut where the Mats are Smoked, New Hebrides	65
Torres Island Nose Ornament	79
Santa Cruz Armlets	93
Plan of Santa Cruz Sea-going Canoe, and View of same showing Sail and House on Deck	96
Nose Ornament, Santa Cruz	104
Ornamented Club, Santa Cruz	106
Club-house, Santa Cruz	109
"He wore Thirty Earrings"	114
A Lady's Costume, Ulaua, Solomon Islands	121
Solomon Island Canoes	122
Ornamented Bowl, Wango, Solomon Islands	127
Solomon Island Sash	129

	PAGE
ORNAMENT WORN ON FOREHEAD, SOLOMON ISLANDS	132
PLATFORM HOUSES, SOLOMON ISLANDS	136
TREE HOUSE, YSABEL, SOLOMON ISLANDS	143
SOLOMON ISLAND STATE CANOE	145
EAR PENDANT, SOLOMON ISLANDS	149
NATIVE HOUSE, NEW CALEDONIA	164

INTRODUCTION.

For the last three hundred years the islands of the Western Pacific have attracted the attention of Europeans to a greater or less extent, but only twice during that period has the interest attached to this part of the world reached the point at which it now stands. The first of these occasions was doubtless when the intrepid Spanish navigators returned home after the discovery of the Solomon Islands, and the second when that extraordinary phenomenon, the South Sea Bubble, was exciting the imagination of all classes of the community.

At the present moment the possibility of our becoming the sovereign power in the Western Pacific has once more directed people's attention to the South Seas, and I am therefore hopeful that the following chapters will supply something of a "want," as the prospectus of a new newspaper would have it.

Of the island of New Guinea—which, indeed, might almost more reasonably be called a continent, considering its enormous size—I hesitate to speak more than slightly, for I have never been there; and were I to attempt to describe it within the same cover as my chapters on the Polynesian groups, I might rightly be accused of mere bookmaking. Having, however, passed the Torres Straits and sighted some of the outlying islands, and having heard so much, almost upon the spot, concerning that most interesting of the remaining unknown portions of the world, I may perhaps include New Guinea in such preliminarily descriptive remarks as I propose to make in this chapter.

As geography is untaught in our public schools, or was in my own time only a few years ago, I may perhaps be allowed to ask my readers, before going any further into the details of a book on the Western Pacific, to glance at a chart of the Southern Hemisphere.

Of the three continents that appear either wholly or in part upon this chart, Australia is the most isolated and unfamiliar. South Africa, with its everlasting disturbances and distresses, is after all, like another unhappy country that might be mentioned, only too near to us; and South America, though less well known, seems but a continuation of North and Central America, which, by reason of West Indian mails and Atlantic liners, have become almost our neighbours; but Australia has an unique position, lying away out there by itself, with its queer-shaped animals, its bark-shedding trees, its interior deserts, and mysterious unexplored territories.

However solitary and self-contained this continent may appear, one finds on looking a little closer that from the north-west of it, right round to the south-east, there may be seen a chain or series of outlying islands. Taking these in their order, we notice first of all Timor—the Ultima Thule of Netherlands India; the last of a series of what, in the old sailing-ship days, when Dutch commerce in the East was at its best, was a magnificent row of strategic positions, guarding, like another Gibraltar, the western entrance to the Pacific. Of Netherlands India I do not propose to write, seeing that such connection as it has with our empire belongs rather to the far East than to Australia; but I may, without going further, be permitted to express my admiration for what has, taking everything into consideration, been a very fair and just administration of a colonial empire, and one that will compare most favourably with anything that Spain, Portugal, or even ourselves, have done in the way of colonization.

Immediately to the eastward, across the Arafura Sea, which is dotted with a few unimportant islands, we come upon New Guinea, the largest island in the world, with an area half as large again as the entire German Empire, and with a population, a vegetation, and possibly a mineral wealth, which, in such descriptions as we have of them, can only be compared to the accounts which the old navigators were wont to bring home in the days of Sir Francis Drake and Salvation Yeo.

New Guinea appears to have been discovered in 1526 by a Portuguese navigator named Menenis, who came upon it quite accidentally whilst making for the Moluccas. It was afterwards sighted and touched at tolerably frequently by vessels on their way to the Philippines or to China, but no attempt was made to explore its coasts. Torres, who gave his name to the strait between New Guinea and Australia, contributed very considerably to the earlier exploration of the island; he landed at many points, but made no attempt to penetrate inland—indeed, the interior of New Guinea is to this day altogether *terra incognita*.

The history of European exploration upon the island is a singularly disastrous one. Schemes of colonisation and exploration have been mooted and even carried into execution time after time, but in nearly every case they have met with total failure. If I except Mr. Chester—the indefatigable magistrate of Thursday Island, who was commissioned by the Queensland Government to proclaim the annexation of the country last April—no one has to any appreciable extent explored the higher plateaus and ranges of New Guinea.* Even the

* On Thursday, April 4, Mr. Chester, in the presence of thirteen Europeans and two hundred natives, hoisted the British flag, and read the following proclamation :—

missionaries, who have done more than any one else in this direction, have been compelled to confine their efforts mainly to the ascending of one or two of the leading rivers.

The climate of New Guinea is no doubt, as far as the low-lying coast districts are concerned, unmitigatedly bad. I should judge it to be very similar to that of the lower districts of Borneo, Celebes, and Java. We must not, however, condemn the country on this account, for on the high elevation in the interior it is almost certain that health resorts, and indeed thousands of square miles of healthy country, will be found, just as is the case in Java and in the Malay Peninsula. The loftier mountains have already been observed, named, and approximately measured; the highest peak appears to be Mount Owen Stanley, 13,250 feet, and there are three or four other mountains over ten thousand.

"I, Henry Marjoribanks Chester, resident magistrate at Thursday Island, in the colony of Queensland, acting under instructions from the Government of the said colony, do hereby take possession of all that portion of New Guinea, and the islands and isles adjacent thereto, lying between the 141st and 155th meridians of east longitude, in the name and on behalf of her Most Gracious Majesty Queen Victoria, her heirs and successors.—In token whereof I have hoisted and saluted the British flag at Port Moresby, New Guinea, this 4th day of April, in the year of our Lord 1883.—God save the Queen."

Of the marvels of wealth, in the shape of forests of gigantic timber, and plains of richly productive soil, it would be useless to write here. This much, however, must be said, that within this vast country, far larger than any country in Europe but Russia, there abound all those natural attributes which for so many centuries have caused English navigators and merchants to look upon Central America and Brazil as Eldorados.

With the history of America, and the stories of buccaneers, gold-laden Spanish galleons, Jesuit missions, and the like in our memories, can we wonder that the Colonial Governments look longingly towards such a prize? And even if we deprecate such covetousness as this, and are prepared rather to take warning at than to emulate the enterprises of three hundred years ago in America, may we not at least recognise the reasonableness of these schemes of annexation, when we are reminded that this land of plenty is a sort of natural outpost, as it were, to the Australian continent?

From New Guinea, following the chain or series of islands above referred to, we come to the groups which it is the object of the present volume to describe. First of all are the Solomon Islands, an archipelago of great resources, which, although at present practically unknown except by reason of the dark tragedies so often enacted around its coasts, will quite certainly, before long, be regarded as among the most valuable and important of all the South Sea groups. A little further to the southeast we find the Santa Cruz Islands, the New Hebrides (now threatened by the French), and New Caledonia, long since annexed and added to the list of deplorable failures which constitute the French colonial empire. Norfolk Island and the islands of New Zealand complete the cordon which stretches along more than half, and that the vulnerable half, of the periphery of the great continent of Australia.

From the position of the above islands it will be evident to all my readers that the physical aspect of the annexation question is the really important one. So much is this the case, that the movement, although unpalatable to a large number of Englishmen, should, I think, at least be fairly considered, and not hastily classed with the acquisition of coast-line in the region of the Congo, or the absorption of vast areas of useless country such as portions of the Transvaal. This is not by any means an endeavour, on account of some traditional line of Imperial policy, to give check to the aggression of one European power, or to the ambition of another; it is simply and purely an act of self-defence on the part of the Australian colonies, who, I think, would be equally alarmed if it were the Japanese or the Peruvians, instead of the French and Germans, who were showing signs of a desire to settle themselves upon the fringe of their territorial garment. Let us, then, not forget that it is to the Australian colonies that the question is a vital one, quite independent of the attitude of European statesmen; and that, although other reasons may have their weight, and other questions (such as that of labour and trade in the Pacific, for example) may be greatly simplified by the English Government being supreme along the line of Western Pacific Islands, nevertheless, the real and main point to aim at is the evolution of a policy of foresight, so that a coming generation may congratulate itself that there were statesmen of sterling enterprise in these days, who in their wisdom built around the Australian continent a bulwark behind which the commercial and manufacturing Australians of another century may live in comparative ease and safety, none daring to make them afraid.

THE WESTERN PACIFIC.

CHAPTER I.

NORFOLK ISLAND.

NORFOLK ISLAND was the first spot amongst all the islands of the Pacific Ocean that was definitely settled by white men. It was discovered in 1774 by Captain Cook, who reported upon it in his usual accurate and graphic manner. There being no inhabitants, and the island possessing very exceptional natural advantages, it was decided in 1788 to found a penal settlement there in connection with the colony at Port Jackson, in New South Wales. Accordingly, a vessel was despatched for the purpose, and twenty-four souls, under Lieutenant King, were left upon the island to found a penal colony. For the next sixty-seven years, with one short interval in 1805, this little isolated spot in the Pacific was the prison-house of our most desperate criminals. In 1855 the convict establishment was finally abandoned, and in the following year the inhabitants of Pitcairn Island (a mere dot in the Pacific, only four and a half miles in circumference), descendants of the celebrated *Bounty* mutineers, who had outgrown their own diminutive home, were at their own request removed to Norfolk Island. Since their arrival the condition of the island has remained almost unaltered. The Melanesian Mission, under Bishop Patteson, established its headquarters there in 1866, but their advent has not affected the island other than as a pleasant social addition.

Norfolk Island is politically in an almost anomalous position : it is not quite an Australasian colony, but its condition is one of almost as great independence. It is six hundred miles from Auckland, in New Zealand, and about nine hundred and fifty from Sydney, N.S.W. ; and there being no communication whatever of a regular character with either Australia or New Zealand, the people are allowed to go on pretty much in their own way, living in a happy-go-lucky manner as far as government is concerned, but being, from all appearances, none the worse off for that. Perhaps only one other speck of land is at all analogous in position to this little colony, and that is Lord Howe's Island, with its curiously-shaped satellite known as Ball's Pyramid. Both the Pyramid and the island itself are very high and well-wooded. Here, although there are only a few acres of land, about twenty solitary spirits have made their home, and earn a scant living by exchanging their fruits and vegetables with such whalers and other vessels as may give them a call.

In endeavouring to convey an impression of the little colony of Norfolk Island, I cannot perhaps do better than narrate my own experiences during one of my visits there : all other information may possibly be looked upon by my readers as padding, and can certainly be found in a more succinct and accurate form in any of the better books of reference.

Norfolk Island is of most forbidding aspect. There is no shelter round its iron-bound shores : there is no permanent anchorage, and landing is almost always a matter of difficulty. On my first visit, I arrived from Sydney by the Fiji steamer, having arranged to be landed at Norfolk Island on its outward voyage, if the weather permitted. My experience on that occasion was a very rough one, for it was blowing fully half a gale, and even on the lee side of the island, where we ran in somewhat near and fired our gun, the sea was running very awkwardly. After an hour or so a whale-boat came off and battled out towards us through the boisterous sea. She was manned by four splendid fellows, and had at the steer-oar a weather-beaten old mariner, whose very hat inspired confidence. Getting into this boat was a matter of great difficulty, for the steamer herself was pitching and rolling in the wildest way, and a dozen times I thought the whale-boat would have been dashed to pieces under the vessel's quarter. We watched our chances, however, one at a time, and then jumped; a few small bags were thrown after us, and in two or three seconds we were clear of the vessel and comparatively safe. But what waves there were, and how utterly fragile and puny our little craft seemed in that great sea! It was for all the world like the pictures on the Life-boat Association's money boxes! I could not have believed it possible, however, to manage a boat so splendidly : excepting the deluge of spray from the wave's crest, we shipped no water whatever, but rode over mountain after mountain of sea in glorious defiance.

We had been dropped from the steamer fully two miles from the shore, and had a very long and fatiguing pull towards the land. Our troubles, however, we learned after an hour or so, were still all to come; we had the actual *landing* to do yet; this boating in the open sea was mere child's play to the work before us. I think our brave "Norfolker" crew took some delight in indicating the dangers ahead. They were too hard at work and too much out of breath to do more than hint brokenly at what we had to go through, but this they did with dramatic power. As we approached the breakers we could see, dimly, a low stone pier which runs out twenty yards or so, and upon the end of which were many figures watching. Our helmsman now stood up, and the crew lay upon their oars for a moment's breath; then we pulled slowly on, and then rested again. A man on the pierhead was watching the rollers as they came breaking in; for a moment or two we lay rising and falling with the waves, then there was a shout and a signal from the pier, and a "lay to, lads" from the helmsman; the right moment had come, and those great weather-beaten sailors *did* lay to in real earnest. For one moment we half stopped, surrounded by a great seething cauldron of foam, and the next, shot round the pierhead and into smooth water.

There was a small crowd on the shore to welcome us—a quaint crowd of weather-beaten men, and yellow-skinned, black-haired women, and bright girls without stays or stockings, and curious peering boys and children. Through these we made our way to a small stone cottage, and there were refreshed with hot tea and relieved of our drenched clothing. Then away across the island to the Mission Station, where we were most kindly received, and given a cheerful bungalow for our residence.

Upon Norfolk Island there are two communities: firstly, that amongst which we landed; secondly, that of the Melanesian Mission. The "Norfolkers," as the proprietors of the island are called, were brought from Pitcairn Island at the Imperial

Government's expense, and were landed at their new home in 1856. They drew lots amongst themselves for the chief buildings and most valuable pieces of land, and straightway settled down as proprietors of the island and all the old convict

"THE TOWN," NORFOLK ISLAND.

buildings thereon. Each married couple received fifty acres at first, but of late years the marriage settlement has been reduced to twenty-five acres.

The majority live in the old convict "town," as it is called, on the south side of the island. There are vast buildings here, which served as prisons and barracks, and more desolate piles of masonry one

could hardly conceive. The larger ones it was found
hopeless to try to maintain, so these are in ruins,
and look hundreds of years old. The officers' houses,
also of fine hewn stone, and the smaller buildings,
are still kept up, and serve as the homes of the more
well-to-do inhabitants. On several occasions we
wandered through the labyrinths of prisons and
barracks, and were told stories of those dark, melan-
choly days of old. They were the most desperate
of criminals that were sent here, and I am afraid
the history of their lives would form no ornament
to our country's annals. We saw the old gallows
where so many hundreds have been led out to their
doom, and where fifteen and eighteen have been
hanged in a morning. We saw the chapel, too, now
in ruins, where the prisoners all assembled for
prayer and service. There is a raised dais at one
end, upon which a company of soldiers was drawn
up with loaded arms. As we stood in the ruined
chapel our thoughts could not but wander back to
one fatal day, when, some sign of rebellion being
shown during God's service and before His very
altar, the word "Fire" was given, and twenty or
thirty were killed or wounded. What a ghastly
scene—the service stopped, the chaplain hurrying
to the vestry, the officers' wives and children fainting
and crying, and the stern soldiers shooting down
the prisoners in the very house of God! Of such
was the life in those old convict days. I believe no

one could draw too dark a picture. Witness this solemn report from the House of Commons' proceedings :—

"As I mentioned the names of those men who were to die, they, one after another, as their names were pronounced, dropped on their knees and thanked God that they were to be delivered from that horrible place, whilst the others remained standing, mute, weeping. It was the most horrible sight I ever witnessed."—*Evidence of Very Rev. Wm. Ullathorne, D.D.*, 1838 ; *Q*. 267, *Report of Select Committee on Transportation.*

And again :—

. . . "Two or three men murdered their fellow-prisoners, with the certainty of being detected and executed, apparently without malice, and with very little excitement, stating that they knew that they should be hanged, but it was better than being where they were."—*Evidence of Sir Francis Forbes; Q.* 1335, 1343, *in same Report.*

The same sad memories are awakened down by the water's edge, a mile or so from the little town, where is a walled-in plot of land. I have never seen so sad a sight, I think, as this God's acre, neglected and forgotten; its old stone monuments sloping this way and that, and the rank grass growing above the graves. Here a captain's little son and here a colonel's wife, here a mother's new-born child, all lying beneath the green grass in this far-off Pacific island. Here, too, many private soldiers and many officers, who had escaped a hundred dangers only to be laid low at last by a felon's hand. Brief records are on most graves of the nature of the tenant's death: "barbarously murdered whilst in the execution of his duty" occurs many times; but most frequently of all items, "drowned while endeavouring to cross the bar." Graveyards are never cheerful places to visit, truly, but there is a desolation about this forsaken spot, out of the way even there on Norfolk Island, that is beyond all telling.

Norfolk Island is always spoken of as one of the most beautiful places in all the world, and indeed, although the list of most beautiful places is so long, it is not said without reason in this case. Its beauty is not the beauty of the tropics, although it is in a latitude that admits of tree ferns and others of nature's richest decorations. The beauty of the tropics is one thing, but there are sights in our temperate zones that no tropical glories can approach. As I think of nature's grandest spectacles—Brazilian forests, and South Sea islands, and mountains in Malay, and jungle-skirted Andes—I feel that they do not possess the poetic beauty of the English lakes or the valleys of Japan. I remember Kingsley somewhere says that one day there will be West Indian poets and tropical artists as far above ours of the Lakes and Highlands as the scenery of those sunny lands is above our own; but this is, I think, a grave error, as all who have known more than the first wild delight of those intoxicating spectacles must feel. The scenery of the tropics is like its fruits and flowers, too rich, too gorgeous; we are for a time dazzled by its splendour, but the joy passes, and we long for our Highland lochs and English fells. I was walking a short time ago along the shores of Derwentwater, and I felt that no Andes peaks, Himalayan slopes, or tropical forests could delight in the way that those soft cloud shadows delighted me, as they chased each other up the green hillsides or down along the water's edge, blending the soft hues of green and blue into sweet picture-poems.

The scenery of Norfolk Island is like that, nor can the fringes of tree ferns and groups of giant pines destroy the peaceful, quiet English beauty of its valleys and hillsides.

What rides are there among the glades and uplands of that little island! Great reaches here of meadow, cleared of every stone or stump in the old convict days. What lovely paths, too, cut through the dense forest! what gallops one can have along the high cliffs, and in and out amongst the partially-cleared woodlands! The whole island is but fifteen square miles, and yet so undulating is it, and so even mountainous in its small way, that there seems no limit to the number of rides one can take. In the old days, before the great works had fallen into decay, it must have been a demi-Paradise. Fine English-looking roads ran round and about the island, gardens were laid out in almost every gully, the grass was mown upon the hills; in short, the whole place was one large park. Even now, its character is more of a park than of anything else, and I shall never forget our rambles on horseback through the beautiful woods and down the valleys and along the high cliffs, the bright fresh air, the yellow sunlight through the trees, the grand effects of light and shade across the great far-stretching ocean.

It is a queer, simple little community that owns this lovely island: the venerable Mr. Nobbs, whose history has been too often told to need repeating here, is at its head. The men are strong, hardy-looking fellows; but in the women one sees a little of the old Tahitian blood—they fade very soon, and are, roughly speaking, only of two kinds, children and old women. The *patois* of these islanders is somewhat curious; it is that of a race of sailors with the slightest touch of foreign accent.

Life is surely easy enough for these good people; all kinds of fruits and vegetables grow with the maximum results for the minimum amount of labour; and there are pigs, cows, sheep, fowls, and horses upon the island in abundance. Whaling is almost their sole source of revenue, however, for they are incorrigibly lazy, and seem to care nothing whatever for more than meat and raiment. The young men are grand boatmen, being brought up to face all manner of danger from their earliest years.

Perhaps the most interesting feature about these people is their attachment to the island; many of them would not leave it even for a few weeks; their whole ideas seem bounded by the narrow margin of their island shores, and they are most singularly free from all curiosity with respect to the outer world. So much, then, for the rightful owners (by special Crown grant) of the island.*

Another community exists on the island, as I have already said; this is the college of the Melanesian Mission, whose headquarters are now permanently fixed here. A thousand acres were given over to the Mission upon payment to the islanders of two pounds an acre. Upon this land a very complete missionary is placed. The Mission college is upon the model of an English public school, there being seven "houses," with schoolrooms attached, in each of which live a clergyman and twenty or thirty natives of the Western Pacific Islands. In the centre is a large hall, where all

* The islanders are governed by a chief magistrate, who is selected by ballot, and who performs his magisterial functions for a limited period. The only punishment for any offence is the infliction of a fine. Capital offences must be tried in the Supreme Court at Sydney. The £2000 obtained by the sale of land to the Melanesian Mission is invested in Sydney for the support of a doctor upon the island, and for other expenses.

meals are taken, and which is also used as a schoolroom. In connection is a printing-shop, also carpenter's and blacksmith's shops, farm-bailiff's house, farm-yard, &c. &c. Last of all, but most important of all, there is the chapel, built in memory of John Patteson, the martyr bishop.

The system that the Mission has adopted is briefly this: Their vessel, the *Southern Cross*, sails to the islands two or three times a year, and brings back native boys and girls, who are placed in the various houses. Here they remain three or more years, and are taught to read and write, plough and plant, make clothes for themselves, and live decent civilised lives. They are then returned to their islands, either permanently or merely for a visit, after which they are brought back again, and, if promising pupils, are further taught, and finally turned out as teachers or deacons. The hours of their labours are, I think, very sensibly short. They have three spells of three-quarters of an hour each day; also an hour or two for working in the fields; and lastly, two services in the chapel, at which there is not, as with us, any "call over," but at which practically all attend.

The principle of the Mission is distinctly wise— first that which is natural, and afterwards that which is spiritual. They do not attempt to alter more native customs than are absolutely needful to be altered. They do their utmost to cultivate friendly relations everywhere, entering into all the pursuits, pleasures, and troubles of their pupils, with results which are, I think, very satisfactory.

I cannot refrain from describing the native service in the chapel, which is the most impressive sight of its kind that I have seen. The building is of dressed stone, and will last for ages. As far as the interior is concerned it is very beautiful; the pavement is a fine marble mosaic presented to the Mission in memory of a Mr. Freemantle. The stained windows are, however, its greatest adornment: they are six in number, and were designed by Burne Jones and executed by Morris. Nothing can exceed the exquisite colouring of these windows, which certainly are the finest specimens of glass painting in Australasia. The interior of the chapel, then, without entering into more particulars, is very impressive and beautiful. As the bell tolls, the bare-footed islanders walk silently in, each one kneeling at his or her place for a few seconds before sitting down. As the hour strikes, the doors are closed and service is commenced in the Mota (an island in the Banks group) language. The responses are uttered by every one, and I have seen nothing to equal the quiet, earnest devotion of these pupils. The singing is really very good, and in all details the service is identical with the ordinary English Church service, but the attention and devotion of the congregation are beyond all praise.

At the end there is a long pause; not a sound is made; there kneel these two hundred natives after the blessing has been pronounced, and one might literally hear a pin drop upon the marble floor. Then they all rise and steal noiselessly out.

The usual half-holidays are given to the pupils, and cricket and other games are played with some enthusiasm. They also make up large fishing and picnic parties on Saturdays, and wander all over the island in twos and threes, enjoying the luxury of needing no weapons, and being free to wander where they will.

It would be unjust if I did not say a word about the social condition of this little community of two hundred souls. There are no servants amongst them, a purely communist system of life being aimed at. The work of cooking, washing, farming, gardening, and the like, is divided, as equally as may be, amongst the pupils and teachers, from the Bishop downwards, and none is too proud to lend a hand anywhere and at any time. The position of the clergymen to their pupils is absolutely paternal: no long-faced, stern disciplinarianism or hollow-cheeked, unapproachable Christianity; but genial good-fellowship and unrestrained enjoyment in both work and play. They seem, these missionaries, almost to have eradicated the old-established feud between youth and lessons, the boys running off to school with almost as much goodwill and merriment as to their games. Not the least remarkable feature of the whole school perhaps is, that although they live so freely together, men and women, and boys and girls, there is practically no immorality amongst them and but little quarrelling, and I doubt if as much could be said of any community of white people that have ever been brought together in present or historic times.

CHAPTER II.

FIJI.

FROM Norfolk Island, the oldest settlement in the islands of the Pacific Ocean, we pass across eight or nine hundred miles of sea to the Fijis, which, if we except Cyprus, constitute the newest English colony. This group is undoubtedly of great intrinsic value to this country, but its special importance for us consists in its being situated upon the future highway from England to Australia viâ Panama.

The books upon Fiji are so numerous and so excellent, that it would be presumptuous for me to enter into anything like a detailed account of the history of these islands, but as books on Egypt still find acceptance, although as many exist as would form a respectable pyramid, so in the observations of a traveller there may be points worth noting down, even after so much that is historical and scientific has been recorded.

The Fiji group is one of the largest and most valuable in the Pacific. It has been known to the

Western World for more than two hundred years, but, like so many of these Pacific islands, was left unvisited, after its first discovery, for many generations. It was not until the beginning of this century that any real knowledge of the group was acquired.

The archipelago consists of about three hundred islands, with a total area equal to that of Wales. Not more than seventy of the islands, however, are inhabited, and of these the largest and most important is Viti Levu, or Great Fiji. From this word Viti the name for the whole group has been taken—Viti, Fidji, Fiji, Fidgee, Feejee, &c., all being forms of the same word.

Between Viti Levu and the island of next importance (Vanua Levu, or Big Land) lies the little mountainous island of Ovalau, upon which Levuka, the capital of the group at the time of my visit, is situated.

A coral reef runs round the entire island, without which is the ocean, broken and rough under the influence of the strong trade wind. Within the reef is a calm blue lagoon with tiny waves rippling upon a sandy beach. One cannot well, I think, exaggerate the beauty of a coral reef, and I, at least, have no words with which to convey the effect of that glorious fringe of snow-white breakers which ceaselessly thunder upon the coral breakwater.

Levuka is a mean straggling little village of the usual New World order. The houses are of wood, with iron roofs and flimsy balconies. Immediately behind the one long street rise the fanciful mountain peaks that we admired so much on entering the harbour; there is not, I suppose, in all Levuka a quarter of a mile of even reasonably flat ground, and I am afraid no town of any size can ever spring up in so unfavourable a situation. The land is even more "steep to" than at Hong Kong, and it would be, one may almost say centuries, before the amount of labour expended upon our little China colony could be equalled here. This is only one of the many reasons why it was resolved to move the seat of Government to another spot, of which I shall speak later on.

In the streets of Levuka, or rather in its street, for there is but one, the stream of humanity flows up and down all the day long. The merchants and planters pass and repass, transacting their daily business. They are a broad-hatted, coatless, red-sashed, and leather-belted community, glad, I think, to see strangers in their little island home. Their club is a pleasant house with balconies hanging over the water, and cool, open rooms for reading, writing, billiards, &c. They are not a contented community by any means, having more grievances than even an English farmer is entitled to. I have never anywhere been so beset by men with troubles. I was button-holed, and cornered, and "stood drinks," and wedged into chairs, and surrounded at all times by such importunity of denunciation against the powers that were, that I felt as if I were engaged in a Fijian Rye House plot. It would be out of place for me here to enter at all into the subjects of dispute so disastrously prevalent in Fiji. It is quite undeniable that the late Governor's policy is the outcome of a most conscientious regard for the best interests of the colony, and if any one wishes to learn the particulars of the controversy between the planters and the Government, they must refer to the various pamphlets upon the subject that have appeared from time to time.

The second but most important feature, numerically, of Levuka street life is the crowd of natives who pass and repass ceaselessly. These do not hurry to or from their work, but glide noiselessly by with that leisurely dignity so characteristic of native races. The men are dressed merely in the "sarang" of Java and the Straits Settlements, called here a "sulu"; the women also wear a sulu, and occasionally a short chemise. Their frizzly heads need no covering, the hair standing up in a substantial aureole-like mass; the more careful natives, however, wearing a sort of turban made of native cloth, to keep it from wet or dust. This crown of frizzly hair varies in colour from white to darkest brown, according to the time that has elapsed since last it was coated with lime. The most general condition is a rich yellowish-brown, which is not unbecoming.

Of pure Fijian life one sees nothing whatever in Levuka. Even the natives in the streets are mostly from other islands, brought here under the well-known "labour" system.

There is, however, about two miles from Levuka, a charming little native village to which I went more than once, and where one could lose sight of ships and houses, and, for an hour or so at least, hide oneself in a little world quite primitive and natural. Here lives, in native fashion, a young Englishman, whose business is in Levuka, but who prefers this pleasant native village to the poor wooden European cottages of the settlement. Here we sat on one or two evenings upon the cool clean mats, in his well-built Fiji house. Natives were lying all around upon the floor, and a low fire burned quietly in a corner. The roof was dimly visible by the light of the small oil-lamp upon the floor, and as one looked up, dark smoke-stained rafters loomed forth, and spears across the rafters. On one side was the small square doorway, not four feet high, and the large moon cast its rays a little way within, and shone upon the bronze chest and arms of a sleeping servant. Without, the waving palm-shadows and the calm lagoon; and beyond, the breakers thundering on the reef. I have known nothing more peaceful or beautiful. Now and then some dark, noiseless figures would pass along and disappear among the palm trees, and then perhaps, above the distant never-ceasing roaring of the reef, would rise some wild fragment of a native song. A weird yet peaceful home this of the Englishman in far Fiji.

A day or two after my arrival I made arrangements with a native chief, who was crossing in an open boat to Mbau, the little island home of the late King Thakombau, to take me to the large island known as Viti Levu.

We walked away from Levuka, past the very pretty and native-looking Government House, to the village I have spoken of above, and here waited for the boat to pick us up. Whilst lying on the clean mats of a pretty hut near the shore, to my surprise, a negro entered, and we soon struck up a conversation. He was born in Virginia an indefinite number of decades ago, and had been in Fiji for many, many years. He told me that his name was Black Bill, adding with some pride that he was generally mentioned in "the books." He seemed to have visited most parts of the world, and was—as what negro is not?—full of narrative and humour. In his time he had been a kind of factotum of King Thakombau's, and informed me with much pathos that had he served his God as he had served the Fijian king, he would not be mending sails in that village that day. We talked for an hour or so of the Southern States and the war, and Baltimore, where he had lived, and San Francisco, where he had begged in the streets, and London, where he had been in a hospital, and half a hundred other places and subjects. Time is hardly a recognised institution in Fiji, and although we had arranged to start at nine, it was past noon when we finally waded out to our boat.

Sailing down the coast was very pleasant—the sea smooth and blue, high land richly covered with vegetation to the right of us, and the thundering, snow-white surf to our left. The enjoyment of this, however, was but of short duration, for our course lay beyond the sheltering reef, and across half-a-dozen miles of very choppy and unpleasant channel. Our boat, moreover, proved to be a newly-imported one, having arrived from New Zealand but a day or two before. It soon showed its quality: before we left the lagoon the gaff was carried away, and just as we were running for the passage several minor "fixings" came to grief, and we had to anchor. Having patched up the rigging as well as we could, we made a rush forthe opening in the reef. To one who has never crossed a reef before this is a *mauvais quart d'heure* indeed. The men stood up in the bows to look for "patches": the breakers seemed furious both to right and left; on we scudded, however, through the partially broken water, and finally out into the rough open sea. For a moment it was really dangerous, for had our most indifferently-repaired gaff given way again, we must have drifted upon the lee breakers, and one has only to see them when the trade winds are fresh, smashing themselves upon the reef, to know what that means.

For an hour or so we scudded along over the high waves, sometimes almost lost in their yawning troughs. It is never pleasant work sailing in a small open boat when the sea is running high, but somehow it was less pleasant than ever that day, for our chief had gone to sleep after crossing the reef, and I had no confidence in the other men, and did not know in what direction to steer myself. However, we soon began to feel the shelter of a long outlying reef that runs away from the eastern corner of the big island, and in an hour more were again in smooth water, whereupon I indulged in a few minutes' sleep, but was soon roughly roused by a crash, and, starting up, found the sail and rigging utterly demoralised, and the mast very nearly over the side. We had brought up short on a patch, and there lay half out of the water. After the usual hauling and shoving, all of us waist deep in the water, which reminded me of similar experiences on the Nile, we floated once more, and about sundown dropped our little anchor close in-shore at Mbau, the royal island of Fiji.

This historical little island is almost part of Viti

Levu, being only separated by a narrow barely-covered channel. It is about half-a-mile long and a quarter wide, but is as pretty as green slopes and numberless native houses and palm trees can make it. All the families on the island are of more or less exalted rank, and here, most important of all, lives the venerable Thakombau, whilom King of all the Fijis, greatest of known cannibals, most dread of savage potentates. His glory is in these days departed, and his title of King cannot be said to be more than complimentary; he has, however, a very large pension from the Government, and after his fashion maintains some state.*

We were taken on landing to a very clean and comfortable house, where the greatest hospitality was shown us. Our chief was not in his own territory here, being lord of Suva, but he was treated, and I also for his sake, with great consideration and kindness.

There was soon prepared for us a most luxurious evening meal in entirely native fashion, and amongst other dishes were some turtles sent by Thakombau, and a banana leaf full of a delicious compound of plantain, coco-nut, maize, &c. Everything we had was served to us cleanly upon the matted floor, wide banana leaves being used as plates, and plaited palm leaves as dishes. The house was, as usual, an

* Since these pages were written the news of King Thakombau's death has reached this country.

oblong building with thickly-thatched roof and sides; the rafters and roof were crusted over with soot from the wood fire which in Fijian houses burns unceasingly in one corner; the floor was very soft and springy, being made of layers upon layers of mats, commencing with coarse palm-leaf ones at the bottom, and having for final covering the beautifully made white ones for which the South Sea Islands are celebrated. At one end of the room is a sort of dais, raised about a foot from the rest of the floor, and upon this the principal members of the establishment sleep. There are two small holes or windows at this end of the room, through which the pleasant cool trade wind blows refreshingly.

The houses of the well-to-do natives are almost always well-kept, clean, and comfortable; at the doorway there is frequently a hollowed log with water in which to wash the feet before entering, a rough mat being placed beside the log to wipe them upon. Both the doors and windows, as one must call them, have sliding palm-leaf shutters, so that on cool nights they can close all up and be comfortable. I have visited numberless native houses in all parts of the Pacific, but unless it be the platform and tree houses of the Solomon group, I have seen nothing that can be compared with these Fijian ones for comfort.

After our evening meal the inevitable ceremony

of "kava" drinking had to be gone through. Some very clean and fairly pretty girls were brought in, having as little clothes on as well could be, and seated themselves in a row on one side of the hut. Sundry friends of the family also assembled, and in a few minutes we were quite a large and a very merry party. An enormous bowl was taken from its peg upon the wall, and placed between us and the pretty girls. It was a splendid piece of furniture, and had been in the family for many generations; its diameter was over four feet, and a cream-coloured enamel covered the greater part of its shallow surface. It had four short legs and was carved from one solid piece of hard black wood.

The kava, or as it is generally called in the Fiji group, the "yangona" root, is in appearance not unlike a large horse-radish; this is scraped of its soiled outer skin and cut into little lumps, which are handed over to the girls, who put them into their mouths and commence solemnly and methodically to—chew. I know Lord Pembroke has insisted that ruminate is the only right word to use, but, try as I would to surround the process with romance and hide the stern realities, I could not persuade myself that they were doing anything less repulsive or more refined than plain *chewing*. It seemed to me from the first to be a very unbecoming occupation for these dusky maidens, but when they stuffed into their mouths lump after lump of the crisp root, and chewed solemnly on with swollen cheeks and distended eyeballs, I began to think the operation positively frightful. When any one of the girls deems her individual mouthful of the needful consistency, she puts her hand to her mouth, grasps the whole mass and places it into the great kava bowl. Then she rinses her mouth with water and begins again. A considerable number of masses of chewed kava ("blobs" or "dollops" as of mortar they really are) at length accumulated in the bowl, and on to these water was poured until they were well covered. Then a stringy, coco-nut fibre thing, which I felt Thackeray would have compared to old Miss MacWhirter's flaxen wig, "that she is so proud of and that we have all laughed at," was brought, and the contents of the bowl were filtered by being wrung, in a washer-womanly way, through the fibre wig, the more solid parts adhering to the fibre and being afterwards shaken out upon a mat: the liquid in the bowl was then fairly clear and ready for use. The drinking of the kava is no mere convivial pastime; it is almost a ceremony. A beautifully-polished coco-nut bowl was given to me, and into it one of the maidens poured from another bowl the soapy-looking beverage. I winced as I realised that my bowl held a pint and a half, for I knew it was etiquette to swallow every drop. I drained it off, however, at one fell gulp, and, as previously instructed, flung the empty coco-nut shell upon the mat with a spinning motion amidst clapping of hands and deep-toned cries of "Ah mata." It is a most unpleasant beverage to a stranger, tasting as I imagine diluted earth and Gregory's powder would taste.

Being compelled to drink it frequently during the ensuing few days, I found the palate quickly became used to the peculiar flavour, and before I left Fiji I almost liked kava; great numbers of Europeans drink it, and not seldom to excess. I have known nothing but a rather soothing effect from it, resembling that of tobacco somewhat, but the natives undoubtedly become intoxicated with it frequently, although I believe not boisterously so; it usually "goes to their legs," as the phrase is, and they fall down and go to sleep before they become riotous.

Later on in the evening I noticed my first finger had begun to show signs of inflammation, and before an hour had elapsed was rather seriously swollen. I knew it must be from the bite of a venomous insect, and asked as well as I could what was best in such a case. My host, who spoke a word or two of English, said, "Oh! native doctor," and away some one ran. In a few moments the doctor arrived, no hoary old fakir c ninety years, as I had expected, but a very shy and nice-looking young girl of sixteen or seventeen.

She sat down beside me with great solemnity, and for half-an-hour, without speaking or smiling, just stroked, with lightest touch, my finger with her own swarthy one. I confess to being quite cured in the morning, but that the cure was due to the treatment of my pretty physician I neither affirm nor deny. In the morning they gave me a delicious bath of clear water in a large black wooden bowl; I then started to ramble over the island.

One white man lives upon Mbau, which is, as I have said, the historic island of the group; this is Mr. Langham, the Wesleyan missionary, who has been there since the very early days. He was away at the time of my visit. I walked out alone, therefore, in the cool morning, and saw the place where the great feasts were formerly held. The old tree whereon were marked the numbers killed at various carousals was blown down in the last hurricane, but the ruins of the native oven were there, and the great gong or "lali," as it is called, which was sounded before the feasts. These gongs give out a weird but not unpleasant sound, and can be heard at almost incredible distances. The one in question was about five feet long and a foot or so wide; it had a deep rich tone. What scenes have been witnessed within sound of that gong! Not twenty years ago this little open space was the place of rendezvous whenever any great occasion demanded a ceremony or a feast. Not twenty years ago this very same King Thakombau, whom I am to see in a few hours, was the habitual author of the foulest butcheries; this was the scene of their enactment and awful consummation. I tried to call up those dreadful times, and picture to myself the human sacrifice and greedy faces, round the low stone oven; but there were children playing on the grass, and the bright morning sun glistened on the water, and my mind could not realise those brutal days of old.

After breakfast I went to see the native school; this is held in a large low building in the middle of the island; it is built exactly like the other houses, but is much larger. There were about a hundred scholars, ranging from four or five years to grown men and women even with babies. They seemed very happy and bright; girls and boys, men and women all mingling amicably together. The noise they made would, I think, have somewhat astonished an English schoolmaster, but their evident enjoyment of their work, and the entire absence of that feeling of *school*, which is inseparable from the mind of English youth, fully made up for seeming lack of discipline. There were native teachers only, of course, and these took charge of the scholars in what I suppose were classes. Some were dividing and multiplying by 3, 5, 7, 9, and the like; others were slowly spelling out little Fiji words; but all were happy and cheerful, and very evidently thought it capital fun.

Presently they all gathered round one teacher, and, squatting down upon the mats, without a moment's warning burst out into a wild and curious chant. There was no laughing now; their faces were all as earnest and solemn as though it were a religious ceremony. I think, indeed, the words they used were from the Psalms, but the chant itself was purely native. One big handsome girl sang a kind of refrain of a weird and curious nature, and the others joined in methodically. Their time was quite perfect, and I shall never forget the effect produced by their now and then stopping instantaneously; it is done at the most unexpected moments, the sound ceasing absolutely, as if cut off with a knife; then the leader would break out again, and the rest join in with their monotonous refrain. I left them singing, but the sound filled the whole island, and they kept it up for some hours; and wherever I happened to be, the quaint notes of that wild song would break upon my ear.

Later on in the day we were summoned to an interview with King Thakombau. He lives in a house which is in all respects like those of the common people; his garden is, however, more extensive, a sort of avenue of banana trees leading up to his door.

As we entered, escorted by various chiefs of the

island, we saw him lying on a mat at one end of the house; he affected not to notice our entrance, so we sat down by the door and waited for a few minutes.

Presently he aroused himself, and, asking an attendant who we were, called me, and I was led forward, and as it were presented; I said, "Saiandra," the native salutation, and shook—not without a shiver—his cannibal hand. I then sat for what seemed an interminable time going through a sort of conversation, of which I understood but little beyond my own part. I did, however, make out that he asked me about my travels, and how big Russia was, and what I thought of India. It was an absurd farce altogether, this interview, for I half-believe the old villain knows a good deal of English. I could not, with my head full of the olden times, get over a feeling of disgust and anger as I saw him sitting there. I began to picture him passing along the rows of condemned wretches, and marking out those for his own use. Here, in this very room, had he eaten of many a score of human beings, and but a few years ago the roof was hung with the skulls of his victims. There he sat, a hard old man, with a worried, peevish face, white whiskers, and small, bloodshot eyes. His house is plain enough, and just like another, there being no signs of royalty beyond a Hong Kong chair given by the governor, and an old French print of a fair-haired lady, leaning against the wall!

After leaving the royal presence we returned to the house of our host, and before saying good-bye I received a very good club with the marks of two victims, and the small Kava drinking-bowl I had used the night before, which I was given to understand was very valuable, as it had been used for many years by Thakombau.

CHAPTER III.

FIJI.—THE REWA DISTRICT.

FROM Mbau we sailed across to the large island of Viti Levu. After running some distance along the coast, inside the reef, we entered one of the mouths of the Rewa river, up which we rowed for ten or twelve miles. The Rewa is the great river of Viti Levu; it is a very large stream for so small an island, and empties itself into the sea by means of a great number of mouths, like a miniature Nile. It is certainly a fine river, and navigable for little steamers for about fifty miles; upon its banks are the leading sugar plantations of Fiji.

The delta of this river is in appearance the most unhealthy place I have seen anywhere. It is a mass of rank vegetation and muddy swamps, and mangroves amongst the water, and water amongst the mangroves. It is like pictures of central Africa; it is like the river valleys of Ecuador and Columbia; it is like everything that is feverish; and one would naturally say at once that it would be fatal for a white man to live there. Yet, strange to say, there is in all the Rewa district no fever or ague at all, and indeed the whole of the Fiji group is practically without that great tropical curse. How to account for this is surely a worthy subject of inquiry, but one concerning which the medical world has at present left us in utter ignorance. I have seen Englishmen living in Fiji on the borders of almost stagnant estuaries, with the densest and most rank vegetation around them on all sides, with mosquitoes and a hundred such insects infesting the district like a plague. In dry seasons their houses will stand in the very centre of great plains of reeking ooze ; in times of flood the muddy river will rise to their verandahs ; and yet these people are robust and healthy. I have gone from there, and a few weeks later have visited islands in the Solomon group or New Hebrides, where I have found a dry coral soil and high land upon which the pure trade wind blows freshly month after month—steep land, too, from which the rain water is quickly borne downward to the sea—and all this but a few hundred miles from the Fiji group, and in the same latitude and blown upon by the same trade wind ; and yet in these places it is almost death for a white man to spend more than a few months in the year on shore, and practically no one who lives ashore at all can hope to escape frequent and severe attacks of fever. Now, surely, in these days of scientific enlightenment, some reason should be offered to account for this. It is to my thinking an infinitely more vital question than the extent or existence of fields of Bactyræ in the South Pacific.

I was landed at some such "Eden" looking spot as has been depicted above in the evening of the day I left Mbau, and having engaged a native to carry my bag, started to walk to a place known as Harry Smith's, where I had been told I could put up for a night.

Our walk lay across a part of the Rewa delta, and I was pleased to find it entirely native land, owned and farmed by the villagers themselves. It seemed to be very rich soil, and was certainly made the most of by the natives.

We passed little patches of maize, tobacco, yams, kumaras, taro, sugar; then again more open ground, where would be growing breadfruit trees and coco-nuts and lemons and bananas. All these things seemed to be in a flourishing condition, and at every hundred yards or so was a small cottage or group of cottages.

Our path was a mere foot-track, winding in and out among the little plots of land, in many ways as like the paths in the agricultural districts of China as could be. I liked the look of this quiet, peaceful, homely district; the people seemed contented and prosperous, and it was indeed hard to realise that so few years ago this was one of the most dreaded cannibal islands of the South Seas. I reached

Harry Smith's after a walk of seven or eight miles in the cool evening, having seen very much that delighted me, and entertaining quite new ideas about Fiji. Not the least pleasant sight was that of a little native canoe scudding down the river as I walked along the bank. It came so silently, and

FIJI HOUSES.

moved with such ease upon the mirror-like water, that I did not for a moment notice something strange about the two figures in it; as it came nearer, however, I saw that the paddler was a little fair-haired Saxon boy, the other figure was his elder sister, also with long fair hair glistening in the slanting sunlight. Nothing could form a prettier picture ; they were as much at their ease in their craft as any native, and their laughter and happy English voices sounded like music across the water.

I passed the night at Harry Smith's in company with two or three planters and a hundred million mosquitoes.

The following day I hired a boat and a good crew of natives, and pulled up the Rewa to the sugar-mills. The distance was some twenty miles each way, so we had no light day's work before us. We went up merrily enough with the tide, my men pulling splendidly ; the heat was, however, intense.

There are two or three sugar-mills on the upper part of the Rewa, but they are of a most primitive order, and will be very shortly entirely eclipsed by the grand new mills of the Colonial Sugar Company, who are spending £100,000 on the Rewa. This company is prepared to give ten shillings a ton for all cane landed at their river frontage, and expect to crush about a hundred and fifty thousand tons of cane from an area of three thousand five hundred acres. The labour employed upon these sugar estates is almost entirely imported. The natives are brought from the New Hebrides and Solomon groups, and hired by the planters for a three-years term. I was told that they worked on the whole fairly well, and, as I saw them during my few days upon the Rewa, they seemed cheerful and well content. Of the labour system I shall have more to say, however, when I come to the islands whence these natives are collected.

It would be difficult to overrate the beauty of this Rewa valley; it is flanked towards the river's source by a lovely range of mountains, so weird in shape, so exquisitely blue, that I found myself comparing them to the Organ Mountains of Rio de Janeiro. Their brilliant colour was made the more remarkable from the intense richness and fertility of the river basin. For miles on either side are plains of well-cultivated land, laid out in farms bearing crops of sugar, bananas, and oranges. There is a path along each bank, and upon this I walked for miles, enjoying the lovely scenery, and being every hour more astonished at the wealth and prosperity of the Rewa plantations. I could hardly believe I was really in Fiji; it seemed like a land that had been enjoying civilisation and prosperity for years. There were bungalows now and then upon the hill-sides, and flower gardens and orange groves and small settlers' houses by the river-bank, and healthful, bearded colonists smoking pipes at the doors of their thatched houses; and once I even saw a prim English housewife sitting at her doorway sewing at some Liliputian garment, just as one might have seen her in England, fifteen thousand miles away. I was sorry to leave the Rewa, it all seemed so peaceful and beautiful, but my stay in Fiji was to be short, and I had therefore to hasten back to Levuka. I went down the Rewa and across to Overlau in a small iron steamer, which was as exquisitely uncomfortable as soot and oil could make it; the absurdities that little six-ton vessel indulged in while crossing the chopping channel between the islands defy all description.

I must say a word about the very beautiful Government House at Levuka. It is built in a little valley, or "chine," as people in the south of England would call it, about a mile from the town, and is most delightfully suitable to the country and climate. The building is, as it were, an aggregate of one-storeyed houses strung together with balconies. The walls are mostly constructed of thin canes placed close together perpendicularly, through which the air can freely pass; in this respect it resembles the houses of Ecuador and Central America. The public rooms are decorated with native curiosities of all kinds, and in places are hung with "tappa," or native cloth. At one end of the drawing-room is a fine collection of Fijian pottery, which in so many respects resembles the ancient Inca pottery of Peru, that theories as to the origin of the Fijians have been based upon their similarity. It is of a rich brown colour, coarse in workmanship, but good in design, and often exceedingly quaint and grotesque. The floors are covered with Fijian mats, upon which the bare feet of the splendidly-formed and handsome native servants fall noiselessly.

On one evening a dinner-party was given, and I cannot refrain from remarking upon the admirable way in which all the details of that entertainment were carried out, yet there was not an European servant in the room. Behind our chairs stood a row of fine-looking fellows, in white tunics cut low to show their broad bronze chests, who waved great oval palm-leaf fans the whole evening, and amongst those stately figures moved the waiters, gliding in and out, and doing their work as faultlessly as Indian or China servants might have done.

Nothing can exceed the quiet beauty of Levuka upon a fine evening; the air so fresh and balmy, the high, weird hill-tops standing out darkly against the bright starlight sky, the long white fringe of breakers glistening in the moonlight.

The governor had occasion to visit Suva, the new capital, about this time, and accordingly the mail steamer was ordered to take him there on its way from Levuka to Sydney. This gave me an opportunity of seeing what in future will be the most important place in Fiji. In little more than six hours from the time we left Levuka we were running through the reef and into the fine harbour of the future capital. I was several hours on shore, and could not but admit the wisdom of the choice of site. This removal of the seat of Government has met with much opposition, but I am convinced it is a wise measure. The site of the new city is very beautiful; indeed I think it would have been hard to prepare a more healthful or pretty spot than this which is provided by Nature. The mountains of Viti Levu stand out gloriously in the west, and as the sun went down behind them on the evening of my visit, no effects of colouring could have been finer. Of course the greatest advantage in this new capital is its proximity to the sugar district of the Rewa. There will be a good road before long from the capital to the centre of the large island, and the great expense of re-shipping and carrying produce across to the island of Overlau will be avoided.

After a pleasant day on shore, we steamed away through the passage in the reef, and the island of Viti Levu soon began to sink beneath the horizon with the setting sun.

It would be presumption on my part to attempt to write of the resources and possible future of Fiji. Nothing as a rule can be more valueless than the opinions of travellers who visit foreign countries, and after a few weeks' kindly treatment from hospitable friends, go home and write as though they had lived in those places all their lives. I have had a pleasant visit to Fiji. I have spent long evenings talking to its best friends, and listened not a little to the grumblings of its worst enemies; I have spied out the land with such powers of observation as I possess, and have found it truly a land of fair promise.

A very rich country indeed has been added to the British Empire, and it does not require a long residence in Fiji for one to learn that the future must contrast almost as favourably with the present, as these present days do with those of the early pioneers twenty and thirty years ago. The cotton of Fiji has long been known, and will be still more known. The sugar, although as yet only just appearing in the market, has even now become no mean rival to that of Queensland. Coffee is grown with most satisfactory results, and but for the question of labour, would very soon be a great industry. Even tea has been tried with some success. Labour, however, is the great stumbling-block to the colony's progress, but of that I hesitate to speak in this place lest there should be no end.

When walking among those plantations in the great Rewa valley, I could not but feel astonished at what had already been done to make a civilised country of a few savage islands, the most striking evidence of all perhaps being the fact that two Saxon children were paddling their canoe along the river for mere exercise and pleasure, with not a white man even near them, but native villages upon the banks, and naked savages walking along the paths, or paddling home with canoe-loads of yams or other food. This very generation has been to a great extent cannibal, and those same men, who call perhaps "Saiandra" or some such salutation to the English children, had but a year or two ago been praying to their heathen gods such prayers as this: "Let us live, and let those who speak evil of us perish. Let the enemy be clubbed, swept away, utterly destroyed, piled in heaps. Let their teeth be broken. May they fall headlong into a pit. Let us live; let our enemies perish." *

To the Wesleyan missionaries one must in great measure give the credit of this marvellous change, and it would not be just to close this chapter on Fiji without a word in praise of their noble work. No one can deny them the highest admiration. Their work was amongst a very fierce and cruel race, but has been carried on with the greatest courage and perseverance; and to show what terrible things have happened upon the little island of Mbau, and to illustrate one aspect at least of missionary life in the old days, I may perhaps be permitted to

---

* In Fiji a salutation is shouted to the sneezer by the bystanders, "May you live." It is proper to utter a good wish in return—"Thanks! May you kill" (*i.e.* an enemy).

introduce the following lines from Williams' "Fiji and the Fijians":—

"The report soon crossed over to Viwa and reached the mission-house. Fourteen women are to be brought to Mbau to-morrow to be killed and cooked for the Mbutoni people. Mrs. Calvert and Mrs. Lyth were alone with the children. Their husbands were many miles away on another island. The thought of the horrid fate that awaited the poor captives aroused the pity of those two lone women. But what could be done? Amidst such fiendish excitement it would be a desperate thing for any one to venture into Mbau for the purpose of thwarting the bloodthirsty people. Those two noble women determined to go. A canoe was procured, and as they went poling over the flat they heard with trembling the wild din of the cannibals grow louder as they approached. The death-drum sounded terrible, and muskets were fired in triumph. Then, as they came nearer, shriek after shriek pierced through every other noise, and told that murder was begun. . . . Surrounded by an unseen guard that none might break through, the women of God passed among the blood-maddened cannibals unhurt. They pressed forward to the house of the old king Tanoa, the entrance to which was strictly forbidden to all women. It was no time for ceremony now. With a whale's tooth in each hand, and still accompanied by a Christian chief, they thrust themselves into the grim presence of the king, and prayed the prayer of mercy. The old man was startled at the audacity of the intruders. His hearing was dull, and they raised their voices higher to plead for their dark sisters' lives. The king said, 'Those who are dead are dead, but those who are still alive shall live only.' At that word a man ran to stop the butchery, and returned to say that five still lived ; the rest of the fourteen had been killed."

Of such—and there are dozens of similar true stories—was the life of the pioneers in Fiji twenty years ago. In our comfortable English homes we think perhaps too little of what the opening up and settlement of new countries really means. In Fiji to-day one might walk alone without great danger in almost any part of the group, and it is not too much to predict that in another five years these islands will be as safe a place of residence as New South Wales. So much, then, of civilisation has been accomplished in the Pacific during the last quarter of a century.

CHAPTER IV.

THE NEW HEBRIDES.

In the previous three chapters I have endeavoured to give some account of the Fiji and Norfolk Island colonies as I found them during my visits to the Western Pacific. These islands are now part and parcel of the British Empire, and as such no doubt possess a certain amount of interest for every intelligent Englishman. I now pass to groups concerning which the people of this country are very much more in need of information—groups which have attracted a considerable amount of attention during the last few months, and which are likely to attract still more attention in the immediate future. In the introductory remarks at the commencement of this volume I have entered at some length into the importance of these clusters of islands, and will not therefore repeat myself here, but will pass directly to an account of my cruise among them.

On one first of July, the mid-winter of that part of the world, I found myself for the second time upon Norfolk Island. A mile or so from the shore lay the little Mission bark, *Southern Cross*, flying the Royal Thames Yacht Squadron's burgee and the blue ensign. She is only 125 tons register, but carries a little auxiliary engine, generally known on board as the "coffee-mill," which is sometimes useful in a lagoon or during dead calms. This vessel was to be my home for the next three months, and I looked at her from the high cliffs near the Mission Station with considerable interest.

During my previous visit to Norfolk Island, Bishop Selwyn was good enough to invite me to accompany him on his next voyage to the Islands, his intention being to visit not only the Solomons, New Hebrides, and adjoining groups, but also to attempt to effect a landing upon the main island of Santa Cruz, and if possible establish friendly relations with the much-dreaded natives, who had been entirely neglected by the outer world since the disastrous visit of Commodore Goodenough in 1875.

There were several boats plying between the vessel and the shore, taking on board stores—yams, pigs, cats, boxes, baggage, and boys. About forty natives were to be taken down this time to their homes, and I must say forty Cook's tourists could not have made more commotion. Some had pigs, many had cats, all had boxes and bundles, some even had babies! Amongst the number were seven or eight women, who had a little room to themselves abaft our cabin; the boys were all to live together

E

in a large room forward; and ahead of that, again, was a small forecastle for the eight seamen.

We were a merry and very noisy crowd that evening, and did not indeed settle down for some time. I almost doubt if we ever should have done so, had not a fresh breeze sprung up, and the ship being "put by the wind," soon commenced a kind of hurdle race movement, which did more to shake every one into his or her respective place than anything else could have done.

We were five or six days making our way to Nengone (Maré), in the Loyalty group, which was our first place of call. It was my first experience in a sailing ship, and although I am willing to admit that in many respects "sailers" are far ahead of steamers in point of comfort, still, a hundred and twenty ton barque can do more in the way of demoralising one's sea-going capabilities than any steamer in which I have travelled. I was ill all the time—ill, first of all, with a fair breeze; ill, next, scudding along "full and by" six points from the wind; ill, "wearing"; ill, "tacking"; ill, running with a good stiff slant; ill, finally, "hove to" off our destination! Whenever I began to recover, the wind would alter a point or so, and an entirely new motion commence; I was very glad, therefore, of a run ashore after six days, and looked ruefully forward to twelve weeks of this kind of thing.

The Loyalty Islands are low and flat, the outline running in terraces which show most markedly where at different times the sea-level has been. They are very evidently rising rapidly. The pines that cover the leaward side of the island are of the same species as those from which the Isle of Pines takes its name. They are thin, quaint-looking trees, in shape like worn-out pipe cleaners. I believe they are closely related to the Norfolk Island pines, but do not resemble them except when very young. They rejoice in the distinctive name of "Cookii," after the great navigator. The Loyalty Islands belong to France, and are technically part and parcel of New Caledonia. The French interest in them does not, however, go farther than keeping a "Resident" on the island, who periodically endeavours to establish a reputation by bullying the natives.

After running along the coast for ten miles or more in the early morning, we came to a little bay where were some houses, off which we hove to and lowered a boat. When we had made our way in the gig through an intricate passage in the reef, we were met by a number of natives, who towed our boat in and out among the patches in the small lagoon, and finally landed us on a little sandy beach.

We found the people in great distress. Naiselene, their old chief, was dead, and, after the manner of loyal subjects, they were quite inconsolable. The more distinguished islanders had their faces covered with soot, down which the tears ran freely as they related the events of the last few weeks. I never saw a more entirely hideous object than the dowager queen, who must have been nearly a hundred years old. Her hair was perfectly white and very shaggy, her face was covered with soot, down which the grimy tears rolled plenteously, falling upon her old bare shrunken breast. There she stood, bowed down with years and sorrow, the picture of savage woe. Her son had been a fine man truly, and his loss to the island is quite irreparable.

After a few hours, during which we were surrounded by a hundred or more savages of every size and age, squatting upon the ground or lolling about under the coco-nut trees, we were much surprised at the appearance of horses. Upon these animals, which had been imported from New Caledonia, we started to ride across the island, nine or ten miles, to where Mr. Jones, of the London Missionary Society, lives. This group, I should perhaps say, does not belong to the Melanesian Mission, but was given up to the London Missionary Society by the elder Bishop Selwyn some twenty years ago. Our ride was not a beautiful one, the path stretching for the most part across a rather barren coral plain, upon which nothing of consequence grows but coco-nut palms. The island seems to be so young that there has not as yet been time enough for more than a very thin coating of soil to cover the coral rock. After a long ride, for riding over either a coral or a lava path is very slow work, we found ourselves at the top of a steep cliff, below which lay a small strip of land, and then the sea. Upon this narrow strip was the Mission Station, to which we scrambled down on foot.

On my return from the islands some three months later, I was set down here by the *Southern Cross*, and spent five pleasant days with Mr. Jones, the missionary. I will not, therefore, run the risk of repeating myself by entering upon a description of this place here, but will merely say that, after a pleasant hour or so at the Mission Station, we rode back in the cool evening, and shortly after dark joined the ship, which had stood off and on for us all day.

From Nengone we ran northward for about two hundred miles, and in forty hours found ourselves off the entrance of Havannah harbour, in the island of Sandwich, one of the New Hebrides.

This place is marked conspicuously on the charts, and is a favourite place of call for men-of-war and traders. It is indeed a splendid natural harbour, formed by a deep bight in the land, across the entrance to which lies an island. At the upper end is a good anchorage, where we found three vessels and an old hulk lying. One of these was an American three-masted schooner, which had put in to repair her rigging, after a lengthened cruise in the northern islands. She had just returned from the Admiralty group, where she had been collecting bêche-de-mer. The condition of this ship's company was very lamentable. The captain had died of all manner of complications on the coast of New Guinea; the mate was unpopular, and the crew discontented and mutinous. I had a long talk with an Americanised Italian, who was in some mysterious way connected with the expedition. He told me that they had been for three months in the Admiralty Islands, and had even lived on shore there for some time, narrowly escaping a carefully pre-arranged massacre. Evidently their negotiations with the natives had been unfortunate, but who could wonder with such a captain and so lawless a crew? It is such vessels as this that sow the seeds of South Sea tragedies, and of the all-prevailing hostility between the natives and white men.

We went on board the hulk, which turned out to be what was left of a French frigate called the *Cheviot*. She had been loaded with "trade" for the islands, but had been dismasted and reduced to her present condition by the late hurricane. We found such a splendid stock of trade on board, that we bought up beads, knives, tobacco, turkey-red, looking-glasses, axes, &c., &c., to the extent of £35!

We landed later on, and found a couple of traders living near where the ships lay at anchor. Their stores, one flying the American, the other the

English flag, were tumble-down shanties, the contents of which consisted chiefly of cheap liquors and rusty old rifles.

From this place, which I suppose is the town of Havannah harbour, we walked three miles along the shore to the Mission Station. The island belongs, spiritually, to the Presbyterian Missionary Society. At the Mission we found Mr. and Mrs. Macdonald and three little fair children; they all looked delicate, and I thought low-spirited. Their work here is indeed not very encouraging; there are but thirty or forty natives around them, and although they had been here eight years, Mr. Macdonald told me that he had never penetrated more than three or four miles into the interior of the island. The little native village looked clean and pretty, however, and in front of the missionary's house was a pleasant garden sloping down to the white coral-sand beach, where the tiny waves were tumbling musically.

There have been several attempts to settle this island of Sandwich, or Vaté, as the natives call it. Australians and Germans have been here, and have cleared acres of bush and landed sheep, but, as far as I can learn, the experiment has been abandoned of late, and is now regarded as almost hopeless. The hills that surround the harbour are very beautiful, and one could hardly wish for a more peaceful picture than this land-locked bay afforded, as we glided slowly out with a light breeze in the evening sunlight.

From Vaté we steered northward again, passed Mae and Api, and through the passage between Mallicollo and the great volcano of Ambrym, and so on to the island of Aragh or Pentecost. I should very much have liked to land at Ambrym, and find out something definite about the volcano there. From the appearance of the sky above the mountain, it has been thought that possibly this crater may exceed in size even the great Kilauea of Hawaii. No white man has, however, made the ascent, and the natives are utterly unconquerable in their dread of the place. They have the same superstitious awe as the Maoris have of Tongariro, and indeed as the Hawaiians had of Kilauea before the missionaries overcame their fears. The ascent is, moreover, from all that I have heard, of great difficulty, and even if one had the time and native co-operation, it would probably require a Whymper to reach the summit.

The island of Aragh is long and narrow, running due north and south. The hills are as much as two thousand feet high, and clothed from base to summit with the most luxuriant vegetation. A few villages are scattered along the shore, and at the extreme north of the island is a little open bay, into which we ran, and let go our anchor.

When a vessel has a number of native passengers on board, one operation is periodically necessary, to wit, "yamming"; that is, taking in stores of yams, the staff of life in the South Sea Islands. At this little village on the island of Aragh we resolved to go through this operation. Two boats were lowered, and a plentiful supply of knives, tobacco, axes, &c., was stowed in the lockers. Then we pulled in to the edge of the reef, which is here merely a "fringing reef," and only a few yards from the shore. Hundreds of naked ruffians, knee-deep in the water, surrounded us in a few minutes, and then such a babel arose as I had not thought possible out of Egypt. It was not that they all spoke at once, but that they all shouted, yelled, shrieked at once!

Each man or woman had a small "kit" of yams, and for these we paid according to their size. There were some ill-looking fellows amongst them truly, and the people here have not a good name, for two boats' crews were cut out a few miles down the coast during the previous year, and several lives taken. Care had accordingly to be exercised to prevent any disputes or over-excitement. Of any excitement beyond what prevailed already, I was, however, unable to conceive.

When we had purchased several boat-loads of yams, the people calmed down a little, and we struggled over the jagged and cruelly sharp boulders of the reef, and so reached the shore. The village is not upon the beach, as one would expect—indeed, we seldom found houses down by the shore upon any of the islands—but is perched up on the top of the cliffs, and is reached only by a rugged and very steep path. These island paths, by the way, in wet weather—and it is always wet weather—are simply agonising. The continual passage of bare feet up and down reduces them to the condition of a glissade, in consequence of which the booted European comes continually to ignominious grief. There were maize and yam plantations on the hillside, upon which a very considerable amount of labour must have been expended. I shall not say anything here about the houses or villages upon this island, as they are in every way similar to those upon the one we next visited, and having had more time there, I shall do my best to describe what of New Hebrides home life I had the opportunity of seeing, when I come to a short excursion I took upon the island of Maewo.

The view from the hill-top was magnificent, and we spent some hours at the little village overlooking the sea. The men and boys for the most part carried bows and arrows, and I induced some of the boys to display their skill with their toy bows. The arrows used in this case were tipped with a blunt lump of coral, and with these they can very skilfully knock over small birds without killing them. I did not see any men shoot—their shooting constitutes a rather more serious affair as a rule; but they should be good shots, as they carry a bow from very infancy.

CHAPTER V.

MAEWO AND OPA.

OUR next stopping-place was on the northern end of Maewo, which is an island very similar in shape to Aragh; its chart name is Aurora. Here is a double waterfall formed by a most lovely stream. We lay nearly three days at anchor off the little river's mouth, and bathed and washed to our heart's content, and filled up the ship's tanks with clear, beautiful water.

There are no villages or houses near the watering-place; we accordingly started, as soon as the work of watering the ship was over, for a short excursion to the villages on the high table-land in the centre of the island. Our walk, as usual, commenced with a very steep and difficult ascent; numbers of natives had come down to see the vessel, and these formed an escort for us on our way to the interior.

There is no island amongst those that I have seen in the Pacific to surpass this island of Maewo in natural beauty. It is indeed an earthly Paradise, and I despair of giving any right account of the glories of our walk that day. The steep hillside up which we climbed was covered with a beautiful convolvulus-like creeper, between which and the black fern and moss-sprinkled rocks we made our way. Now and then, at a turn in the zig-zag path, there would be an opening in the wall of creepers, through which, while resting a moment or two, we could gaze out upon a beautiful scene of blue sea and distant isles. I shall never forget the delight of leaning back against the moss-covered rocks in the deep, cool shade, and looking across the path at these lovely pictures with their flower frames.

At the top of the path the view was of course more extensive, but it was far less enjoyable; the strong sun could shine through the forest trees as it could not through the wall of creepers. The sea lay spread out before us like a great sapphire carpet, but it did not look so perfect as in those little creeper-framed pictures that were hung for us along the gallery of our ascent. The path we had come up by was literally a gallery cut in the rock face, as are the passages in the rock of Gibraltar, but the defence afforded was not that of live rock against an enemy's cannon-balls, but of thick walls of bright green foliage against a burning sun.

Proceeding on our way, we found the path level and pleasant for the next few miles. It wound in and out through the forest—now under a great banyan tree, which we roughly calculated must cover nearly two acres; now along the river-bank;

now through the river; and so away towards the centre of the island.

After about four miles' walk, we came, quite suddenly, upon a good-sized village. It was the most pleasant and unexpected sight. Instead of the usual little cluster of squalid huts among the

A NEW HEBRIDES VILLAGE.

trees, we found a wide clearing, quite level and free from either grass or weed: perfectly clean, moreover, so that one could not so much as see even a coco-nut shell lying out of place. Sprinkled, as it were, upon this level clearing were about a dozen little houses. Some of them were fenced around with white cane fences, but all had planted beside the doors one or more handsome flowering shrubs or trees. It was—to be horribly commonplace—like a fairy scene in a theatre: the ground was so clean, the colours so bright, the little houses so smart and toy-like! Some of the flowering shrubs, planted purely for their beauty's sake, were really magnificent—great scarlet flowers on one; cream-coloured honeysuckle blossoms upon another; bright yellow bell-shaped flowers upon a third. Alas! not one of us was botanist enough to know the names or families of these flowers, and although some of us had been in many countries, we could not compare more than a few of them to any we had seen before.* The leaves of many of the trees were no less beautiful than the flowers, and I

---

* By "we" in these chapters I always mean Bishop Selwyn, one, or at times two, of the Melanesian clergymen and myself. Both Bishop Selwyn and Mr. Bice have spent one or two weeks on this island. With this exception, no white man has probably been beyond the sea-board. Neither the traders, nor indeed the officers, from such few men-of-war as visit this part of the Pacific, care to go inland, or out of sight of their ships. The inland tribes are generally hostile and almost always distinct from the coast tribes : hence complications are liable to occur. Although I cannot claim to have been the first white man at any of these islands, I earned the title, laughingly bestowed upon me by the members of the Mission, of "the only unarmed layman," which I believe to be truthfully applicable to me as regards every landing that I effected !

have seldom seen a more gorgeous display of crimson, gold, and brown foliage.

The houses are small, and have, strictly speaking, no walls. They consist of a deeply-gabled roof set upon the ground, and are, in fact, like very large and long hen-coops. The workmanship is, however, as I have said, very neat and good. A small square doorway, perhaps two feet high, leads into the single room, and the floor is covered with rough mats. There were very few natives about the village, the greater number being away at work upon their little plantations. I did not think them a good-looking people by any means. They are very naked, the men wearing merely a small banana leaf stuck into a string round their waist. The women wear nothing whatever in the ordinary way, but many, in consequence of what the missionaries had taught them, when we appeared, donned a leaf or strip of calico if they had it. Naturally, however, the women of all ages on this island are entirely nude, and even express great unwillingness to wear any covering, pleading bashfulness, and that they are ashamed at being made so conspicuous! Upon the island of Opa, only a few miles off, on the other hand, one never sees either a man or woman without a little finely-woven mat for covering.

Passing through this hamlet, we followed the path for a few hundred yards, winding as usual through the forest, and then came upon another level clearing sprinkled with houses, and after that another and another. This is the way the people live; their villages are aggregates of little villages, the inhabitants of each hamlet being as a rule connected by birth or marriage.

To each village is attached a club-house, or "gamal" as it is called. A club system prevails throughout almost all the Western Pacific Islands, varying merely in detail. When the boys of the village have grown out of actual childhood, they are sent from their homes to sleep and eat in the village gamal, which is generally in a central position. Upon entering the club they pay a small fee, and sleep and eat at what is called the lower end. From this position—which may be compared to the lowest rank in a Masonic lodge—they work their way gradually upwards, at each advancement paying the chiefs of the club-house certain fees. The gamal is generally thirty or forty feet long, and divided up into small divisions, there being, however, no actual partitions, but merely palm logs laid on the ground. There are two or three bed-places in each division; bows and arrows hang above the beds, and a wooden bowl or two upon the wall. The gamals that we visited were as a rule empty, with the exception, perhaps, of an old chief at the upper end, who was too old or too dignified to go out to work.

In connection with the fees paid for advancement

in these curious lodges I must not forget to mention a curious custom on this island. Of course the money is different in every group of islands, just as in every country of Europe, but here it is so singular that it deserves special mention. Near the centre of the village at which we stopped was a small and rather exceptional-looking house. It was fenced around, and had a more elaborately-constructed

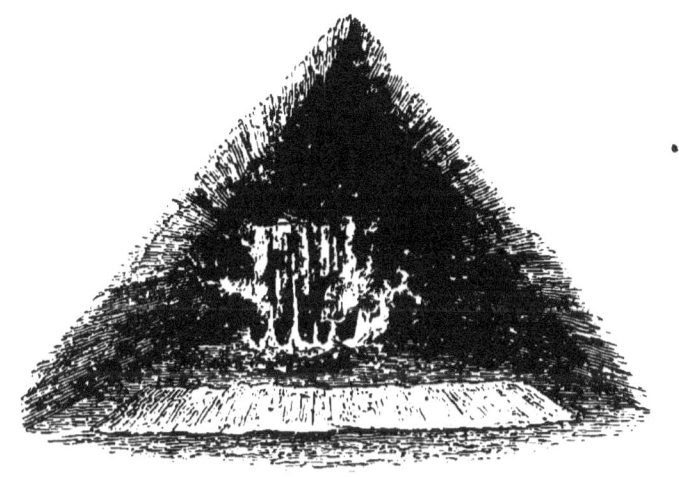

INTERIOR OF HUT WHERE THE MATS ARE SMOKED.

front than the common dwelling-places. This we learned was the money-house. We were taken to see what was inside, and crawled through the very small doorway for that purpose. From the roof of the hut were suspended eight or ten mats, their sizes as they hung down from the beam being about two feet by fifteen inches. They reached to within a foot of the ground, and under them a small wood fire is kept ever burning. In course of time the mats become coated with a shining black incrustation, which gradually accumulates in such a quantity that it hangs down in stalactite forms, called by the natives "breasts." The fire, it will be seen, requires very constant looking after, for if it became at all large the mats would be set alight, and if it went out the process of coating them would be arrested. A man has therefore always to be kept watching these curious moneys, and it is the time thus spent upon them that makes them of value. This kind of money is, as far as we could learn, only current in the matter of club advancement. A fairly old mat is worth as much as a large boar with finely-curved tusks. Of all the forms of money that I have seen this is certainly the most curious, for it cannot be carried about, and is never moved even when it passes from one owner to another.

The people here had built a very clean and pretty little house for the use of Mr. Bice, the missionary, during his visits, and we had the most favourable account of their advancement in decency and civilisation. Only a year ago, when the Bishop was at this place, they buried a woman alive, and it is still a very common occurrence to hear of an old creature being killed off when any one is afflicted by the loss of a child or a parent; but they are gradually giving up these customs, and never allude to them without shame. The burial-places of these people are most beautiful as well as singular. They build a little wall, say a foot high, of stones round the grave, and plant the enclosure with the most beautiful flowering trees and shrubs they can find; thus the graves are like little flowery plantations scattered about on the cleared plain of the village, and are peculiarly picturesque. All the small hamlets we passed—and these were very many—were alike prim, clean, and tasteful. They are really model villages, and the care bestowed upon the trees and shrubs is beyond all praise.

The path that we followed back to the coast was even more beautiful than the one by which we came. We crossed the river—which lower down forms the waterfalls—many times; crossed it at lovely little pools and tiny cataracts enclosed on every side with steep and creeper-hung rocks. These pools and little waterfalls were gems of scenery. In two places we discovered terraces, the steps and basins of which are identical in form with those of Rotomahana in New Zealand. The formation here, however, is not silica, as at Rotomahana, but a very similar substance of a grey colour. The interest attached to the existence of these terraces lies in the shape of the basins and the overhanging character of the steps, from which, if the theory of the deposition of the New Zealand terraces, as described by Mr. Abbay* before the Geological Society in 1878, be correct, it is proved that the water at the period of their formation must have been hot. This idea is confirmed by the fact that lower down the stream, where the water would have been cooler, although the deposit still fills the river basin, the terraces give place to a mere inclined plane. In one or two places, notably in one known as *the* waterfall, this plane becomes exceedingly steep, yet so tenacious is the deposit left by the water, that, although not without much difficulty and even danger, we were led by our native guides right down the fall on foot, the rushing water, ankle deep, adding to the difficulty of the descent. The sensation was most curious, for had the ground consisted of any other material, our feet must have slipped. When we reached more level ground, we passed through numerous yam plantations, and also taru fields. Taru is grown, like rice, under a few inches of water, and the irrigation works in connection with these little patches were very elaborate, resembling those of the paddy fields in China.

I visited only one other island of the New Hebrides group, namely Opa, or Leper's Island. It is magnificently mountainous, and stands out of

* *Vide* a paper in the Quarterly Journal of the Geological Society, May 1878, upon the building-up of the white sinter terraces of Rotomahana, by the Rev. R. Abbay.

the water to the height of 4000 feet, its outline resembling in shape a whale's back. We visited Opa on three occasions, and lay at anchor on the N.W. or leeward side of the island. The people are better-looking than those of Maewo and Aragh. The women are very elaborately tattoed, the designs covering the whole of their bodies like those of the coolies of Japan. Some of the men wear their hair in numberless oil-soaked ringlets, like those of the ancient Egyptians and the Nubian women of to-day. The females in almost every case had their hair cut short, after the manner of our convicts. None of the people on this island are naked, the women wearing a short skirt, and the men a narrow native mat passed between the legs and tucked into a waist-string before and behind.

The condition of Opa just now is peculiarly deplorable, as several "cutting out" cases have recently occurred, and the action taken by the Commodore and the High Commissioner has not as yet produced any satisfactory results.* We visited the small village where Johnson, a white

---

* Since the above was written, accounts have reached the English papers of a visit paid by H.M.S. *Miranda*, from which, even after allowing for the usual inaccuracy of such news, it appears that some very definite punishment has been inflicted upon the perpetrators of the *May Queen* and other massacres.

trader, was shot a few weeks previously in cold blood; the people, however, seemed friendly enough, and many assured Mr. Bice that if any attempt at hostility were shown they would stand by him. We found one poor boy lying under a banana tree in great pain, and almost breathless, suffering from acute inflammation of the lungs. We put a hot yam poultice on his chest, and covered it over with banana leaves. He was very quickly relieved, and when we called again, eight weeks afterwards, appeared quite well as far as his chest was concerned, but had severed his large toe with a tomahawk, and this had been neglected so sadly that mortification had set in; so I suppose the poor fellow will have died after all. In the club-house at this village were many bows and poisoned arrows, also a few loaded rifles. The place was dirty, smoky, and out of repair, but picturesque.

We had a long sail back to the ship, and were caught by a squall from the hills, and as nearly swamped as I suppose any of us will be again in our lives. These squalls are peculiarly violent and sudden amongst all the more mountainous islands of the New Hebrides, but perhaps are nowhere more dangerous than at Opa. On this occasion we had taken a boat-load of yams as a present to the poverty-stricken people of the village. It was quite fine early in the day, and on our way there we had pulled against a light breeze with no great difficulty. The return journey, however, was a different matter, for we had not sailed more than a mile from the shore, on our way across a bight in the coast, when a terrific squall caught us, and our boat, being flying light, was almost literally blown out of the water. It was at the height of the squall that our sail jibbed violently, and threw the boat over until the sea poured in green over the gunwale. Of course the native crew were paralysed with fear, and could do nothing; indeed, how the boat ever righted herself again is a mystery. We were all glad when we made out our little vessel through the blinding spray, and not many seconds afterwards were safely hauled in under her quarter.

CHAPTER VI.

THE BANKS AND TORRES ISLANDS.

WE next visited the Banks Island, which lie to the northwards of the New Hebrides. These islands, less known than their neighbours, constitute a small group discovered by Captain Bligh in 1789, during his wonderful voyage to Timor after the *Bounty* mutiny.*

On our way between Opa and the Banks Islands we called at Merelava, or Star Peak, a little volcanic island precisely resembling Stromboli, but which

* The following paragraph, taken from Captain Bligh's 'Voyage to the South Sea,' London, 1792, refers to the discovery of the Banks Islands :—

"The sight of these islands served only to increase the misery of our situation. We were very little better than starving, with plenty in view; yet to attempt procuring any relief was attended with so much danger that prolonging of life, even in the midst of misery, was thought preferable while there remained hopes of being able to surmount our hardships. For my own part, I consider the general run of cloudy and wet weather to be a blessing of Providence; hot weather would have caused us to have died with thirst; and probably being so constantly covered with rain or sea protected us from that dreadful calamity."

has not been active within the memory of any of the natives.

Mota was the first island we visited in the Banks group. It is the headquarters of the Melanesian Mission in these seas, and is chiefly remarkable on account of its language, which is probably the most perfect of any dialect in the Western Pacific. The Mota language has been adopted as the vernacular for the schools at Norfolk Island, and all the boys, wheresoever from, are taught Mota, not English. The people on shore were very glad to see our vessel, and came down to the rocks in hundreds to welcome us when we landed. There is no water on the island, which is the greatest drawback to its advancement, and although the Mission has visited it for the last seventeen years, the appearance of the people is exceptionally disreputable.

Upon Mota Lava, a larger island a few miles away, we found a white trader living. The place is healthy and pretty, the soil being of light sand. This trader had been some months on shore collecting "copra," and seemed very contented and happy, having with him his Samoan wife, who kept a neat little house, where I had some tea. My hostess could talk a little English, and gave me a fan from her own island, the handle of which was made from the butt end of a ramrod, as a memento of my visit. In the adjacent village I found nothing especially worth mentioning, except, perhaps, that the chief seemed to be so big a swell that the club-house literally could not hold him, so he had erected at the end of the long low "gamal" a small but very elevated little shrine for his own individual use!

I will put down here a few notes of Banks Island customs, which are very similar to those prevalent throughout the New Hebrides, gathered from time to time from my companions.

A marriage is generally arranged between the relatives of the pair interested, a payment being made to the father, who will then give up his daughter when it is thought desirable. There is no ceremony, but sometimes a feast is arranged at the time of the settlement of the affair amongst the relatives. When the day arrives for the bride to leave her father's house a present is usually made to the son-in-law. Girls do not go about alone, and it is not an uncommon thing for them to remain chaste until marriage.

In cases of adultery the injured man may either kill the offender or beat the wife. It is generally customary for a man to have two wives. A man will not name his wife's father, but will sit and talk with him; he will not come near his wife's mother, nor mention her name—they avoid one another, but if necessary will talk at a distance. A man will not name his wife's brother, nor his son's wife; and hardly any one in any of the islands can be induced to mention his own name. In Fiji, and also at Opa in the New Hebrides, brother and sister are strictly tabooed, and will not even speak with each other. If people from old age or sickness are lingering in misery it is usual (of course except where the missionary influence has made itself felt) to bury them alive. This is sometimes done when relatives are tired of nursing the sick, who are not unfrequently buried with their heads only uncovered; their friends going from time to time to ask if they are still alive. Cannibalism is utterly unknown in the Banks group, although universal throughout so many of the other islands in these seas. There are regular terms upon which property may be borrowed; the rate of interest is cent. per cent. without any limitation as to time.

We called at Vanua Lava, an island with the same name as the second island of Fiji, and also at Santa Maria, the most southern of the group. This last place is interesting in many ways. It is almost circular in shape, and about twelve miles in diameter. In the centre, some two thousand or so feet above the sea, is a beautiful lake, lying as it were in the old crater of a volcano. The people have been long known as treacherous and warlike, but of late years have behaved themselves more peacefully. An outlying reef runs round the island, through which we ran in one of the ship's boats.

On the weather side is a pretty little village, to which I walked through a mile or less of beautiful forest. On account, as we were told, of the number of pigs kept by the people here, the houses are built upon massive foundations of stonework, and are really of imposing appearance. The pigs certainly are numerous, and this place is celebrated for its boars' tusks, which are used so largely for armlets amongst the Banks Islands and New Hebrides. Scattered about the village were small store-houses raised some feet from the ground upon piles, and identical in every respect with those used by the Maoris of New Zealand. The main feature of the village, however, consists of a long stone wall running right through the group of houses, and ornamented at intervals with large wooden images carved from palm trunks. Other similar images were grouped about near the houses. They are very grotesque and rude, and are said not to be idols, but monuments in honour of deceased chiefs. The arrows of this place seemed to be more than ordinarily deadly, as on several occasions, when I wished to buy some, my boy from the ship, who spoke a word or two of English, warned me with the statement that they "makee kill allsame musket."

Coasting round to the leeward side of the island, we passed some very pretty scenery, notably a point known as "Cocksparrow Point," although why so named I did not learn. Here it was almost always usual for the boats to be shot at until quite lately. Upon this promontory is a curious cave, shaped like a short bottle, with only one outlet, namely, at the top, resembling in this respect the cells constructed upon Norfolk Island for exceptionally dangerous prisoners. Concerning this cave is an amusing native legend, which was told to the Bishop, and runs somewhat as follows :—

THE LEGEND OF THE GREEDY BIRD-CATCHER.

Once upon a time many warriors went out from the village to shoot birds and fish for their families and themselves. Some wandered by the shore and some upon the hills, and so, each pursuing his own course, they became scattered and separated. Presently one chief, walking by himself, came upon a hole in the ground, which he discovered to be a cave, and in which were many hundreds of birds. This chief was a greedy chief, and did not call to any of his friends, but went back home and told nobody. In the evening, when no one was watching, he stole away to the cave with a rope, determined to let himself down and catch many birds. This he very successfully did, but on reaching the bottom the rope fell down after him, having become unfastened from above, and he was made a prisoner. It was useless to call to his friends now, for all were at their homes in the village, and no one was at all likely to be within ear-shot. Thus he remained in the cave many days, and his friends thought he had been killed by a shark or by some hostile tribe. Then, thinking he must surely die, he became very despondent. Presently an idea struck him, and he set vigorously to work pulling the loose rope to pieces and making it into a great number of short strings. When this was done he took his bow, and with some blunt arrows he had, soon knocked over many of the birds, which were so plentiful that he could almost catch them with his hands. These birds he tied to his limbs in all directions, leaving their wings free. Then, when he had got a large number tied to his arms and legs, and all the string was used up, he made as great a noise as he could, and plunged and kicked about as much as his exhausted strength would allow him. This so frightened the birds that they all at once made a dash for the hole in the roof of the cave, and so strong were they, and so much frightened with the noise that he made, that they flew right out through the hole, taking him with them; and so the unfortunate but selfish man, after a severe warning, was saved!

We glided away from Santa Maria upon the most peaceful of evenings, and in two more days were at Lo, one of the smaller of the Torres Islands. This group consists of four little low-lying islands to the north-west of the Banks. They are, geologically speaking, of recent origin, and strikingly resemble the Loyalties in outline. We called at only one of them, the vessel not having been here more than once previously. I believe it is the intention of the Mission to pay more attention in future to the group. We made two visits, one on the way north and the other on our return, when we left Bishop Selwyn behind to stay two months with the people, who were suffering most acutely from horrible sores, aggravated by want of water and careless treatment.

The islands of the Torres group, as well as several of the Banks, are practically altogether without water. The soil consists of crumbled coral, through which the rain percolates as it would through sand: the natives are accordingly dependent upon coco-nut milk as their sole beverage, and of course do not wash. At Mota, in the Banks Islands, as I have mentioned above, the effect of this want of what we consider a necessity of life, was very distressing, but upon the island of which I am now writing it was positively appalling.

TORRES ISLAND NOSE ORNAMENT.

The men wear a short stick, generally about

three-quarters of an inch in diameter and an inch and a half long, through the cartilage of the nose, which presses the sides of the nostrils upwards, giving a most hideous expression to the face. These little blocks are of polished black wood, and have a small mother-of-pearl disc let into them at each end.

We found a very large number of people on the coral rocks which surround the little inlet where we determined to land. Their appearance was far from inviting, as they were very well armed with bows and arrows; on further acquaintance, however, they proved to be amongst the most amiable and merry people we had met.

There have evidently been many labour vessels here from time to time, for we found that several men could speak a little "sandal-wood English," as it is called; none of them, however, appeared at all pleased with their experience of civilisation. The place they had been to was Port Mackay in Queensland, the centre of the sugar district. One man was very communicative, and had a long sentence such as the following, which he repeated continually—poor fellow, it was the only thing that remained to him of his three years' wages: "Me speakee English, my name belong Black John, me been Porter Mackai, too muchee wark, my word, me no sleep all er time, plenty wark, big fellow wind he come, me plenty sick, my word, me no likee Porter Mackai, plenty sugar he stop, me carry him plenty time, me get one feller bokus (box), one feller gun, plenty tambacca, me stop three feller year, my word too muchee wark, me no sleep, me carry sugar, my word, me no likee him, now you give me tambacca, you come England? me savvy England, plenty far, good feller man he belong England, feller man belong Porter Mackai he no good." And so on, over and over again.

When we landed on our way south seven or eight weeks later, we found the condition of things very deplorable. We walked up to the village with a long string of natives carrying the Bishop's boxes, &c. They had promised to build a new house, but had been unable to do so. The terrible sickness was striking them all down. The usual straggling hamlets are to be found here also, connected by a winding path through the woods; at certain places all the women and girls filed off down a different pathway from the one we took, ours being tabooed for women. They were a bright and merry lot, but it was terribly sad to see their little villages in the state they were. The houses are simply semi-circular arches built upon the ground. I have never before seen the semicircle taking the place of the gable in native architecture. Outside almost every hut we saw a little temporary shed, and here lay the sick from the house. I have seen nothing more horrible than this disease; it generally attacks the legs, and flies and want of water soon produce mortification, and the sufferers die; and yet the wonder in most cases was that they *lived*, for so awful was their appearance we really could not look at some of them. All the time as we walked along, our communicative friend kept pointing to little graves, with the words: "Here two man he stop. Here three feller man. Here woman stop;" and so on. The malady seems to be contagious, and there was some little difficulty about our visit, for these people are very superstitious, and would easily persuade themselves that the white men had brought the disease.

We tramped along for a short distance towards the centre of the island, surrounded by the usual crowd of wondering natives. Many of them had doubtless never seen white men before, for such labour vessels as have been here would not have sent any one inland. The young girls and boys were very pretty and affectionate, holding our hands as we walked along. Nothing seemed to strike them so much as our *nails*, men and women being called up repeatedly by the more courageous ones to look at and feel them. When I first pulled up my sleeve there was quite a stampede—that any one should be white all over seemed to them something quite fearful! Towards the end of our visit we discovered an amusing fancy which we had not understood before; it was that the people were all most curious to know our names. I had been asked some question a hundred times, and at last some one guessed what it was that they wanted. After that Bisopé (Bishop) and Kooti (my name) were passed round with huge delight and much pointing at the possessors of these titles!

The Torres Island people, although I fancy thick-headed and merry, have at least the art of making very beautiful arrows, which are small and of a light-coloured wood, highly ornamented. Their bows are perfect pieces of workmanship too, and they also make tortoise-shell knives, like paper knives, for eating their food with; but this is about the sum of their industries.

One really needs to visit some such place as this to appreciate the value of water. Here were many hundreds of men, women, and children, of whom I suppose but a few had ever known what it was to wash. Natives will not use salt water to wash in, although they will bathe in it while fishing, or even perhaps for pleasure. On the whole, however, these dirty Torres folk seemed to me more merry than any people I visited, and the noisy crowd that came down to see us off was evidently none the less happy for being so unclean. It was only when we saw the poor dying wretches, lying in dozens outside their houses in miserable little sheds, that we realised how awful a thing it is to be the prey of disease and flies and loathsome insects, in a tropical country and without the all-purifying element.

We sailed from Avava, as the Torres group is called in its own language, northwards to Santa Cruz, leaving these poor creatures in great spirits at the prospect of the Bishop's return, when we were to leave him behind us on our way south.

CHAPTER VII.

THE SANTA CRUZ ISLANDS.

IN 1567 Don Alvaro de Mendaña sailed westward from the port of Callao to find still more new worlds, to carry still farther the Castilian standard, to add if possible still more to the already so long list of Spanish discoveries and conquests.

The expedition crossed the great Pacific Ocean, steering always toward the setting sun, and for months the bold navigators sailed doggedly westward, always hoping for a reward. Their voyage was even longer than the journey from Europe to the New World, but with the memory of Cortez and Pizarro in their minds they were nothing daunted. At last they discovered a group of large and beautiful islands, and finding at the southern end of them a well-sheltered bay, they anchored and commenced an examination of their newly-acquired possession. We are told that "the discoverer of these islands named them the Isles of Solomon, to the end that the Spaniards, supposing them to be those isles whence Solomon fetched gold to adorn the temple at Jerusalem, might be the more desirous to go and inhabit the same."

Mendaña's published descriptions of the islands were full of magnificent exaggeration. The land was of unparalleled wealth; even Peru was not comparable to it. Here were not arid mountains and forbidding deserts; here was a very Paradise, where every kind of valuable wood abounded, as in Central America, where Nature was most prolific in her gifts, where gold was plentiful and water plentiful. We can well imagine the descriptions those ancient mariners would give when they returned to the simple country folk of their native land; all their hardships were then forgotten, and nothing remained to them but vague memories of the distant islands, so often enlarged upon that now even they themselves would not know truth from falsehood.

The outcome of these extravagant stories was what might have been expected. Volunteers were soon found willing to venture even so far as to these Solomon Islands, in the very uttermost part of the earth; and twenty years or so after his return, Mendaña again started from Callao at the head of a small band of adventurers, who had determined to settle in these newly-found Pacific islands. Westward steered the great navigator as he had done before, and in due time picked up an island which at first seemed both large and beautiful, and which no doubt was thought by all on board to be one of the group. Mendaña soon discovered that there was some mistake; this was not one of the Solomons, nor had he even sighted this land on his previous voyage. A discontented mood, however, took possession of his followers, who determined to stay where they were, and, seeing that the islands were fertile and well-watered, to attempt the formation of a colony. The description of Mendaña landing is so characteristic of all the early efforts, whether of Spaniard or Englishman, to approach newly-discovered natives, and also affords such a striking parallel to our own experience, excepting as regards the last two sentences, that I give it as it stands in Burney's Travels :—

"The *Gapitana* and the *Galiot* being near the north coast of Santa Cruz, there came from the shore a small canoe with a sail, followed by a fleet of fifty other canoes, the people in them calling out and waving their hands; but they approached the ships with great caution. When the canoes drew near it was discovered that these people were of a dark complexion, some more black than others, and all with woolly hair, which many among them had stained or dyed with white, red, and other colours, and some had half of the head shorn; other distinctions were observed, and their teeth were stained red. . . . . Most of them were stained or painted black, so as to make them blacker than their natural colour. . . . . They continued for a time irresolute. At length they set up a loud shout, and sent a flight of arrows at the ships. The Spaniards, who had kept themselves prepared, fired their muskets in return, and killed one Indian and wounded many others."

The opposition which the natives showed to the landing of the Spaniards was very soon overcome by the force of musket and sword, and a settlement upon the main island was rapidly pushed forward. The accounts of this little colony are of the highest interest, though very brief. The Spaniards apparently pursued the same tactics as they had done in the West Indies and in South America, but here the natives were of a very different order, and the history of the colony is a consecutive record of disaster and bloodshed.

Mendaña himself died on the main island in October 1595, and partly on account of his death, and also, doubtless, from the hostility and ferocity of the natives, the grim conquerors who had faced so much, abandoned, apparently for ever, all idea of extending the Spanish power so far afield. They returned disheartened to Callao, and the Santa Cruz group of islands was no more seen or heard of for over two hundred years.

They were rediscovered and visited by both Carteret and D'Entrecasteaux at the end of the last century, and a few names were given to them, and the principal bearings of the islands were laid down. Nothing, however, of interest, beyond the ferocity of the natives and the excellence of their canoes, was recorded until twelve years ago. In 1871 the group was brought conspicuously before the public on account of the terrible tragedy on the

THE SANTA CRUZ ISLANDS.

small island of Nukapu, where Bishop Patteson and others were killed. The incidents of that murder are too well known to require repetition here: there is little doubt now that the affair was carried out in deliberate revenge for the kidnapping of five natives which had taken place some time before. In 1875 the English public were again startled by the news of the murder of one of the most popular commanders in the naval service. On that occasion, as I believe has always been the case, the natives seemed both good-natured and friendly until a moment before the party left the shore, when, without the slightest previous warning, an attack was made upon the party, and Commodore Goodenough and two seamen were wounded with poisoned arrows. The Commodore died of tetanus on the ninth day, and both the sailors who were struck also lost their lives. Since this sad event the islands have been almost left unvisited, no attempt whatever having been made to land.

Towards this group, of so curious and fatal interest, we directed our course after leaving the Torres Islands, and soon found ourselves in sight of Vanikoro, the southernmost island. The group takes its name from the large or main island, which was first called La Isla Granda de Santa Cruz, and whose native name is Nitendi or (as in some dialects) Ndeni. It consists of about a dozen islands, some eight of which are quite small, and lie to the north in a cluster known as the Swallows or Reef Islands; next to these lie Nitendi, and to the south, again, Tapua and Vanikoro. It was upon this last-named island that the celebrated expedition of La Pérouse—the Franklin of the Southern Seas—was lost. One could hardly conceive a more dangerous piece of land, for from every corner of it run great reefs, giving the coast a most forbidding appearance. As we sailed along the coast I watched the breakers from the fore-top-gallant yard, and they seemed to stretch away in every direction like the feelers of an octopus. Although the island is itself quite small, the circumference of the reef is estimated at no less than thirty-five miles.

Several European traders have been at this place during the last few years, mostly attracted by the report that there were still valuable remains of the La Pérouse expedition upon the reef to the southwest of the island. The ill-fated Capt. Ferguson, who was murdered three years ago in the Solomon group, succeeded a year or so before his death in obtaining an amount of salvage, in the way of brass cannons, &c., that was, I believe, sold in Sydney for as much as £600. The natives are reported to be friendly, and no doubt white men will be attracted here before long.

It was not our intention to call at Vanikoro, so

we stood away, after running close to the reef, and brought up the following morning off Tapua, which lies some twenty miles to the northward and westward. Here we intended to call, as H.M.S. *Basilisk* had been in some years before and had found a good harbour. We stood off what was evidently the harbour's mouth early in the morning, and even lowered a boat to try and find an entrance through the reef. After several hours, however, we were obliged to give up the attempt, for the wind did not serve so as to secure us a good retreat, supposing we got into any difficulty. We stood away again, therefore, that night, and passing to the eastward of the main island, brought up in the morning off Nufiluli, one of the Reef Islands, which the Bishop had visited two years before.

These Reef Islands of Santa Cruz are small low coral patches, I suppose nowhere more than thirty feet above the sea level. They lie in a very labyrinth of reefs which have never been explored. We backed the main-yard in a narrow channel between the islands of Nufiluli and Pileni, and allowed the fleets of canoes which were paddling from the two islands to come up to us. The natives came alongside quite fearlessly, for they knew the vessel—as well they might, since the Bishop had brought back to them in 1878 a man from here who had been blown away as far as the

Solomon Islands, and whom he found a prisoner there. They were very excited, for no vessel had been seen by them since the Bishop was here before, over two years ago. This man was amongst the first on board, and very glad he seemed to see his old friends. Before long the vessel's deck was crowded with the natives, who swarmed up the sides like monkeys. They were finely-made fellows of a dark copper colour. Through their noses they wore a thick tortoise-shell ring about an inch and a half in diameter, and in their ears were from ten to as many as twenty thin tortoise-shell rings of about the same size. A very fine and neatly-made mat was their sole article of clothing, passed between the legs and tucked in before and behind in the same manner as those worn by the natives of Opa in the New Hebrides. For ornaments the usual armlets were worn, and also in many cases a round flat shell breast-plate was hung round the neck. Most prominently of all, however, they carried, always and without exception, large redwood bows, and from a dozen to twenty long and highly-ornamented poisoned arrows. Their canoes were quite laden with sheaves of these arrows, which are certainly the most terrible and deadly weapons I have ever seen. They are not (indeed no arrows in these seas are) feathered like our own, but are made of a simple cane shaft four or five feet long, and carved with some care, the designs upon them being coloured with red and white pigments. The points are long and thin, and of a light brown colour, the tips being made of human bone.

The canoes of this group of islands are as distinctive in character as the people themselves. They are almost always *built;* that is, are not carved out of a single log, as is usual in the canoes of less

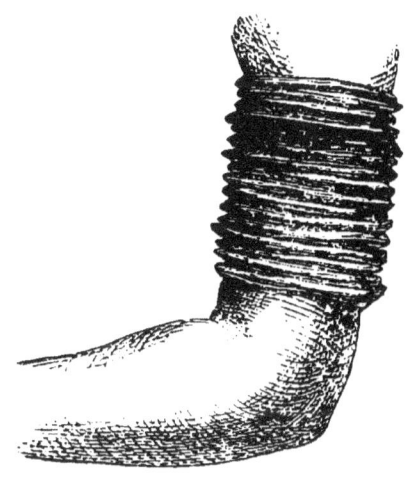

SANTA CRUZ ARMLETS.

ingenious races. They are, moreover, stained white, and in addition to the usual outrigger have a counterbalancing platform on the other side, on which may be carried bundles of arrows, coco-nuts, bread-fruit, and other necessaries. Their dexterity in the management of these canoes is most remarkable. We saw several of them upset and swamped, but the owners, swimming up to them, would, in less time than it takes to write of it, shake the water out with a swinging motion, jump in, and bale them dry with the greatest ease.

After an hour or so, during which we ingratiated ourselves into the good opinions of the natives as much as possible, we resolved to go ashore. The Bishop had landed on the small island of Nufiluli before, and we had but little fear of hostilities here, the only element of danger lying in the jealousy which exists between the natives of Nufiluli and the island of Pileni, a few miles to the north. Whenever any attention was shown to a chief of the former island, the natives of the latter seemed displeased, and *vice versâ*.

We pulled up in the whale-boat to the opening in the reef, surrounded by many canoes. There was but little water in the lagoon, and dozens of natives had waded out waist deep fully two miles to meet us. I never saw a more beautiful reef formation than exists at this place. Outside, the sea is profoundly deep, say eighty or ninety fathoms, and one can look down through the sapphire-coloured water into an apparently infinite profundity. From these depths the coral wall rises perpendicularly, as though built by human labour. But what human labour could compare with this? Walls of Baalbec or Saracenic traceries, or Campanile of Giotto, or Roslyn Chapel pillars—the greatest or most beautiful of man's creations, what are they to such a work of Nature? I have seen a thousand wonders of human skill, patience, and ingenuity, but this little island wall, built by the never idle though short-lived coral architect, puts every one to shame. There is no describing it—no conceiving its wealth of beauty. There it stood, perhaps five hundred feet from base to summit, faultlessly pure and beautiful. Through a narrow cleft, I know not how many hundred feet deep, in this wall, we steered our boat, and soon were in shallow water, among the coral patches of the lagoon. We were pushed and towed through the shoal water for about two miles before we finally ran the boat upon a sandy beach, and waded ashore.

Drawn up upon this beach were some splendid canoes, fitted with spars and sails, and reserved for long journeys. They were over forty feet long and were decked in, so that such cargo as they might carry could be battened down and kept from wet. Upon the platform between the main hull and the outrigger was a small house in which a fire could be lighted. The sail, which was of matting, was of the usual heart shape, with a semicircle cut away from the top. These vessels will not sail near the wind, but attain a very fair speed when running free. The natives of Santa Cruz do not hesitate to make cruises far out of sight of land, their knowledge of the stars being very considerable. I have noticed the elder of the three boys whom we

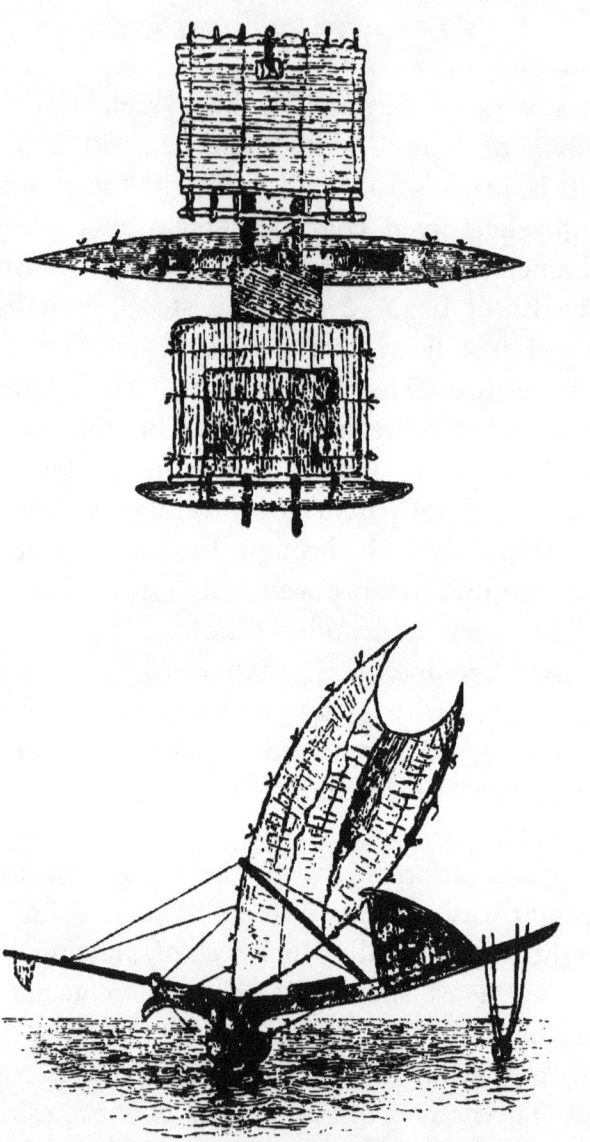

PLAN OF SANTA CRUZ SEA-GOING CANOE, AND VIEW OF SAME SHOWING SAIL AND HOUSE ON DECK.

subsequently brought away with us from here teaching the names of various stars to his younger companions, and was surprised at the number he knew by name. Moreover, at any time of night or day, and in whatsoever direction we might happen to be steering, these boys, even the youngest of the three, a lad of ten or twelve, would be able to point to where his home lay. This I have found them able to do many hundreds of miles to the south of the Santa Cruz group.

Upon landing we found a number of natives on the beach, with eager and curious faces, but as yet there were no women visible, and we were taken up at once from the shore to the club-house of the village. There appears to be no great difference between the club system here and that of the New Hebrides. The house, however, was larger and better built than any I have seen in the more southern islands. The floor was covered with mats, and a finely-plaited one was brought for us to sit upon. The leading men of the village sat all around, and hot breadfruit and yams were brought for us to eat. We had with us a Loyalty Island native, who had been left here for a few months two years before, and he was able, to a certain extent, to act as interpreter. We were perhaps an hour in this house undergoing a sort of examination, and being looked upon with immense delight by the less dignified of the community. My beard was so generally admired that friends were continually brought in to gaze at and even to stroke it, after which they would depart in great glee, and communicate the result of their experience to small knots of idlers outside. From the club-house we were taken by a chief to his private residence, where we again were seated upon mats, and brought presents of breadfruit, &c. This house was one of a small cluster, and a stone wall ran round it. Here we saw for the first time many women and children. The girls were finely made and of strong and healthy appearance ; the children very shy, but with the invariable bright, pretty eyes.

They were laden with tortoise-shell earrings, and all the men and boys wore the thick ring through the centre of the nose. In this chief's house were four divisions, boarded off by partitions three or four feet high, and having the appearance of stalls in a stable. Each of these loose-boxes, as they may be called, was the sleeping-place of one of the chief's wives, who, when a stranger enters, promptly repair to their quarters, and remain until wanted. In some houses we saw as many as six of such divisions.

After a tedious repetition of the process of being stroked and admired, we walked about a mile along the shore, under a fiercely-burning sun, to another small village, and here went through some more sitting in state, being presented, moreover, with bags of nuts, kits of breadfruit, coco-nuts, and yams. Whenever any gift was made a return present of very much greater value was evidently required. Blue beads are the rage in these islands, and with them practically everything the natives have may be bought; also small pieces of iron, eight inches long and one and a half wide, are in great request. These pieces, the value of which is about a penny each, are preferred even to finished axes, and I think the reason of this must be that they can work the raw material into whatsoever tool they may find most suited to their purpose. But what labour it represents—grinding by hand, upon a rough stone, short sticks of iron into useful tools!

Of the things to be bought, mats are the chiefest, and some of these are very beautifully executed, being made almost exactly in the way so-called "sword mats" are made in civilised countries. We also bought some of their money, which is curious. It consists of coils, resembling a very old leather strap an inch wide, which are covered with scarlet feathers neatly sewn on, and are worn round the waist upon state occasions. I was unable to obtain a new one, nor indeed did I see such a thing. Such as we bought were evidently of great age, the scarlet colour of the feathers being visible only when they were lifted up. Models of canoes also were offered us for sale, and one that I saw was almost large enough to hold a boy. They are evidently made as toys for the children.

After a very wearisome day we managed to get clear of the beach; getting away is always the difficult thing in such cases as this, for every one wants to come in the boat, and when ordering them out or pushing them over the side, one may very easily commit some breach of etiquette and get into trouble. At last, however, we succeeded in launching the boat into deep water and pulling away.

We had accomplished the object of our visit, which was to induce some of the natives from here, who were known at a village upon the main island, to come over with us, and as it were introduce us to the chief there. Elated with our success, we pulled off to the ship in good spirits, accompanied by dozens of canoes, which, however, by hoisting our sail, we soon were able to leave behind. I remember that one white-haired old ruffian, with the most diabolical countenance and not a rag on his body, stood up in his canoe and shouted so pathetically to us that we lowered our sail for a moment and waited for him. He came paddling up breathlessly, trembling with excitement, and seizing the Bishop's hand with great fervour, he rubbed it carefully with his nose; then he very formally presented me with the oldest and most disreputable poisoned arrow I ever saw, and paddled quite contentedly away! There are eccentric characters evidently even at Santa Cruz, and we laughed very much at the grotesque behaviour of this veteran. To be on board the old ship again was a great relief, it seemed so homelike and safe. Never on shore for a moment had man or boy laid down his bow or bundle of arrows, and we could not but feel that it would have required very little at any time to have occasioned a disturbance.

CHAPTER VIII.

SANTA CRUZ.—THE MAIN ISLAND.

WITH six natives of the Reef Islands on board, we made our way during the night towards Nitendi, the main island of Santa Cruz. We kept well away from the shore, in order to avoid being seen by the coast tribes, until we believed ourselves to be opposite the place at which we hoped to land, when we bore directly down upon it. It is a bold, high island, this of Nitendi, very different in appearance from the newly-formed coral islets to the north, and appears to have no outlying reefs whatever. We got up steam in our little "coffee-mill," so that in case of any trouble with the natives we could at any rate insure the vessel "staying," should we require to beat off the shore, and also to a certain extent retain command of the ship if the wind fell light. Passing the place where Commodore Goodenough was killed, we stood in towards an open bay a mile or so to the westward, where is a small inlet and a village known as Lelouova. For some time we had noticed canoes paddling about even as much as four or five miles from the land, but none ventured near to us, and we stood on our course, steering straight in towards the little bay. As we got nearer the number of these greatly increased, and at last we sent our Reef Island natives, who knew some words of the language of this island, into the rigging to shout to the men in the canoes. These natives, who had in their own boats visited the place for trading purposes, soon made themselves understood, with the result that a few of the more bold spirits ventured alongside. No sooner had this been accomplished than, leaning over the bulwarks, and enticing them with beads and "turkey red," we induced a few to come up on deck. By this time we were as close in as was deemed wise, and therefore backed the yards and lay to. Hundreds of natives soon swarmed up the side, and they seemed even a wilder and more uncouth-looking lot than those of the islets to the north. I can conceive of no more repulsive objects than were some of these men; let a copper-coloured savage shave his head in parts; let him gather up such of his crisp woolly hair as is not cut, into long, frizzly tails, which will stand out like spokes from the boss of a wheel; let him dye some of these white and some scarlet as his sweet fancy may direct; let him smear his face with charcoal, relieving the monotony of soot, however, with scarlet or yellow streaks; let his body be scaly like a fish's, from skin disease, and yellow in parts from the wearing or carrying of turmeric-coated mats; put a thin mat between his legs, and a large round shell plate upon his chest; squeeze a dozen pearl shell bangles upon the upper part of his arms, and hang a ring through his nose and twenty in his ears, not forgetting to smear his big

NOSE ORNAMENT, SANTA CRUZ.

ugly mouth with the red juice of the betel nut; let him carry always and everywhere some twenty thick arrows, highly carved, tipped with poisoned human bone, and painted red and white; add to this interesting bundle a long red bow, and perhaps a richly-ornamented club;—and you have the makings of a pretty considerable ruffian! Not one whit less terrible in appearance than this description implies were many dozens of the men that now swarmed upon the decks of the *Southern Cross*. Some of them were fine, good-looking young fellows, gorgeously arrayed in pearl armlets and tortoise-shell earrings, and wearing elaborately-fretted mother-of-pearl plates fastened into their noses, which partly hid the centre of the face. There were also white-headed and closely-cropped old villains, with countenances little short of demoniacal in their ugliness; and all were in a state of excitement which I should have thought beyond possibility. Every canoe was well stocked with bundles of poisoned arrows, some of which we were able to buy with beads and iron.

There is something about the appearance of these bundles that is more terrible, I think, than that of any other weapons. Their colour and high ornamentation; the smooth long points of human bone, which presumably are steeped in some deadly juice so that the faintest scratch shall produce tetanus and death; the horrible stories connected with these arrows; the universal fear of them, resembling that of hydrophobia;—all these things lend a ghastly fascination to the arrows as we see them in every man's left hand and piled up in dozens upon the outriggers of the canoes.

Nearly every man carried a small sack resembling the "old clo'" bag of the London streets, although not so large, and in this he kept the little stores which he brought off for barter. We were offered more mats than anything else, and some of them were perfect in taste and workmanship. Clubs also were brought—not the polished hard ones that one ordinarily sees, but a curiously-shaped white kind, with designs upon them painted in red and black. The eagerness to sell was something beyond all describing; at times, seeing in one of our hands something they would like, perhaps half-a-dozen men would leap from their canoes and struggle up the side, so overcome with excitement that they could hardly even shout, their faces being absolutely awful to look upon.

This kind of thing lasted an hour or so, and then Mesa, the chief of the place, and probably also of this part of the island, came off in some state. The Bishop received him in the cabin, and resolved to accom-

ORNAMENTED CLUB, SANTA CRUZ.

pany him ashore. A boat was therefore lowered, but it was not thought safe for any one to go except the Bishop and the Loyalty man, who had spent some weeks upon the Reef Islands two years ago. Twenty natives jumped into the boat as soon as it touched the water, and then the Bishop squeezed himself into the stern in the midst of them, and shaking out the little sail, steered towards the land. We arranged meanwhile to keep as many natives on board the ship as possible, and to signal if there were any sign of them clearing off for the shore. It was very nervous work, for no one had been here since September 1875, when punishment was administered to the natives on account of the murder of Commodore Goodenough.

In half-an-hour or so we made out the boat coming off again to the ship, and soon the Bishop was alongside, and reported that every one on shore seemed friendly, and that he proposed leaving the Loyalty Island man here for a time, calling for him again in about two months. This man, whose name is Wadrogal, is one of the elder Bishop Selwyn's earliest pupils, and possesses a large share of the bravery for which all the natives of the Loyalties are celebrated. He expressed himself quite willing to stay, and even to take his wife on shore also; such things as he might want therefore being put into the boat, the Bishop sailed in again, and this time I jumped in among the wild naked crowd, and was taken ashore also.

We landed upon a steeply-shelving shore, consisting of iron sand such as is found on the west coast of New Zealand. There was a good deal of surf breaking upon the beach where our boat grounded, and into this we immediately plunged, waist-deep, hoping to steady the boat by holding on to the gunwale. A great many natives were on the shore, standing by the bows of the boat, and we expected these would have helped us to run her up out of the breakers: they did not lend us a hand, however, but merely shouted and gesticulated. This was rather an awkward moment, and I began to wonder what would happen next; we could not haul the boat up ourselves, and the natives did not seem willing to help, but surrounded us in great numbers, vociferating and making signs, we all the while not understanding a syllable, but struggling to keep the boat from bumping.

After a few rather anxious moments, the mystery was solved—a long line of women appeared. Here were the labourers; these lords of creation could not stoop to pull or carry. We soon got all we wanted done with the help of the women, although they seemed very frightened.

Mesa, the chief, who on board had evinced much partiality for my society—partly I fancy on account of some turkey-red on my helmet, which, however, I had deemed advisable to leave behind me—now that the boat was well out of the water led me affectionately away from the beach, evidently with the desire of showing me something.

We passed by some splendid canoes, even larger

CLUB-HOUSE, SANTA CRUZ.

than the ones we had seen on the other island, and so away from the beach along a small pathway through the forest. This took us after a short time to a village in which was a fine club-house (called an "ofilau"). Here I went through the usual sitting in state and eating hot breadfruit and being admired. There were not many people about, as the ship had attracted a large number, and many more were with the Bishop by the boat. Several men, however, sat down with me, and numbers of boys peered in at the low doorway. We were intensely jovial and noisy, talking and laughing a great deal, although not understanding a word of each other's language. Unbuttoning my shirt, I caused the most unbounded delight by the exhibition of a white chest, and when I kicked off a shoe and displayed a foot of the same colour, the excitement and astonishment knew no bounds. People flocked in to see and touch the strange creature, and their wonder and curiosity rose higher than ever. I had brought with me no presents or valuables of any kind—nor indeed any clothes beyond the plainest shirt and flannel trousers, as it was most desirable not to excite their cupidity; but I found, fortunately, a small bundle of fish-hooks in the pocket of my shirt, and these I distributed amidst great enthusiasm amongst my crowd of admirers. It was a strange experience, indeed, to sit there, where I suppose no white man had ever been, amongst that crowd of savages, perhaps the most treacherous in the world. The light was dim, for there were only two or three square holes for doorways; a fire burnt in one corner, and in the centre of the house was a large arrangement like a four-post bed, upon the top of which were stored bags of nuts and stores of spare arrows and other treasures. Every one had his bow and arrows, and would not so much as cross the house without them, and I could not resist a suspicion once of foul-play and quickly-roused tempers; it was therefore pleasant to see through the little doorway the waves dashing against the rocks outside, and in the distance the ship with the canoes still round her. After some time we went out again, Mesa still indefatigably attentive, and walked through the village, which consisted of a great number of houses built closely together. The women here were very shy and had an ill-used appearance; I saw one rather pretty girl, but she slipped away timidly as I came near.

Walking back through the forest to the little bay where the boat was, I passed a woman leading a child by the hand, and carrying on her head a black wooden bowl containing mashed yams. She stepped aside, and covered her face with some native cloth that she wore around her, much as an Arab woman would have done. The child shrank away from me in fear, and another one that followed ran crying into the forest. Mesa and his companions laughed contemptuously, but they themselves had been but little less frightened a few hours before on the ship. I walked in front, not, perhaps, without a feeling of nervousness, as I was quite unable to watch the movements of my savage escort. It was a narrow moss and fern covered pathway; there was a little stream of water, and across it natural stepping-stones. The rocks were black, and tree-shadows were thrown across the path, with little bright circles of light sprinkled everywhere. It was like a glade near Bolton Abbey or in Derbyshire, and, but for the loud talking of the natives who followed me, I could hardly realise that this was indeed the main island of the Santa Cruz group, and I almost the first white man that had visited that village and walked along that little pathway.

We found a great crowd upon the beach, and they did not seem at all to like our leaving, but evening was now upon us, and delay would have been most unwise. Amidst great excitement and noise we struggled away from the shore, bundling as many natives as we could into the water, and "casting off," when possible, those who clung on to the gunwale of the boat. These people never seem to realise that there is a limit to the number even a white man's boat will carry.

In an hour or less we had cleared every one off the vessel, with the exception of our six friends from the Reef Islands, and were standing away north-west again, to pay a second visit to Nufiluli and Pileni, and return these men to their homes. I have seldom been more utterly tired—not from actual bodily exertion, but from sheer excitement —than when I got on board the ship again. There was a feeling of relief amongst us all that night ; the anxiety of the last few days was taken off our shoulders now, for the experiment was over, and had proved satisfactory. With such terrible precedents we could hardly have expected so successful an experience. Our best hopes had been realised, and a beginning at least had been made upon an island that had been considered almost hopeless. It is impossible to say what the people thought of our visit, but as we carried no arms and took practically nothing from them, but gave away a considerable amount of, to them, inestimable treasure, one may presume they considered our intentions were friendly. Our success undoubtedly lay in the fact that we came as it were with introductions ; that is, we brought natives with us who already believed us to be harmless and even useful. This very scheme was attempted by Bishop Patteson ten years before. He had been shot at here on the main island, for his motives were misunderstood. He crossed over, accordingly, to the small islands to the north, where he thought the people were more friendly, and landing there in hopes of first making himself known to them, met with his death.

We landed our Reef Island friends at their homes on the following day, and made several visits on shore, the most important result of which was that we succeeded in getting three boys to come away with us. This was almost as great a triumph as landing at Nitendi, for no one had yet been taken from this group. The youngest boy soon became a great favourite on board. His name was Naweo, and a more bright, sharp-witted youngster one

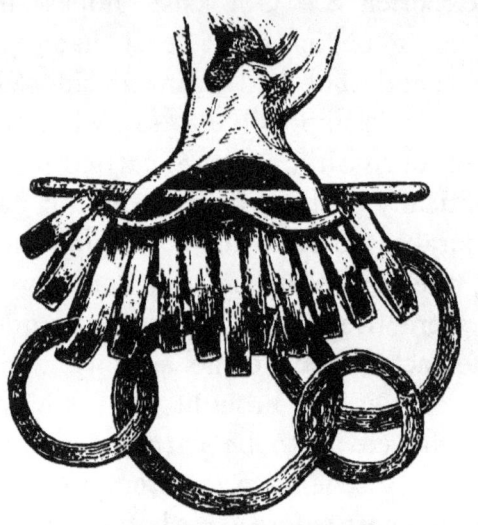

"HE WORE THIRTY EARRINGS."

could hardly imagine. He wore thirty earrings, some of considerable size,* and a nose-ring, and

* The natives of Santa Cruz all use head-rests, many of which closely resemble in shape and size those found in Egypt. These wooden pillows are also common in Fiji and New Caledonia; they are not, however, in these cases used to preserve the hair, as in Japan and possibly in Egypt, but on account of the number of earrings, which make it impossible for these people to sleep with their heads on the ground or upon any other kind of pillow.

although very sea-sick at first, soon recovered, and was for the rest of the voyage, the merriest and happiest of all the boys on the ship. His great accomplishment was the manipulation of a piece of string into what I believe are called "cat's cradles." It is interesting to notice the widespread prevalence of this amusement. The natives are very clever at it, and can carry out very numerous combinations, taking and retaking the arrangements from each other for hours together.

We lay off Nukapu, the island where Bishop Patteson was killed, on a calm, beautiful evening, but no canoes came off, and no signs of any kind were made by those on shore. This island had not been visited for nine years, the last occasion being when H.M.S. *Rosario* called after the Bishop's death, and an engagement with the natives took place.

We made no attempt to land, as it was threatening a calm, and we thought it wiser not to incur any further risk amongst these people for the present.

In the morning we were out of sight of Nukapu and off a small island called Nupani, where the people are apparently friendly, as many canoes came off, and their occupants, after but little hesitation, were induced to come on board. They seemed even more excited about "turkey-red" than their neighbours of the other islands, and I shall never forget the frenzy of delight that was shown when we tied pieces round their heads. They trembled in an agony of expectation before receiving them, and when they had them on, danced and hooted and yelled like maniacs.

Almost all the time during our cruise in this group the volcano of Tinakolo was visible. It is a perfect cone, rising without any fault from the sea level, and while we were in its neighbourhood sent forth a thin and beautiful column of white smoke. On the last night a brilliant stream of fire issued from the crater, and ran down the sides of the mountain into the sea, producing a grand effect like some pyrotechnic masterpiece. What an evening it was, this of our leaving the Santa Cruz group! A light and balmy breeze, deliciously cool after the hot and tiring day; the sea calm and quiet, but with just a slight ripple upon its surface; the stars as clear and bright as on a winter's night in Northern Europe; and away in our wake the grand and mysterious island volcano, with its fire fountains illuminating the southern sky.

From Santa Cruz we stood away to the westward, steering for Ulaua, in the Solomon Islands.

CHAPTER IX.

THE SOLOMON ISLANDS.—ULAUA AND SAN CHRISTOVAL.

THE Solomon Islands will probably be found to be the finest and richest group in the Western Pacific, and although there is not quite the romantic interest attached to them which is felt as regards Santa Cruz, still, the more that is seen of them the more of interest is discoverable. Santa Cruz has borne an ill name in these latter years, and neither the whalers of a past generation nor the traders and recruiters of to-day cared to go near them; hence everything connected with that group is new, and the traveller, when lying off the coast waiting his opportunity to effect a landing, finds himself literally in the position of Captain Cook a hundred years ago, or even perhaps of Mendaña and such adventurers as he.

In the Solomon Islands it is different: half the group has already fallen a victim to the ne'er-do-weels of commerce. Whalers have left their mark in the Southern Islands, and traders and labour-agents have prowled along every shore in search of spoil; the result of which is, that the landmarks of the coast are the records of massacre and revenge, and hardly a bay or inlet exists but can boast its tragedy.

The last twenty years of crime and bloodshed have not, however, done much to alter the fact that here is a land which hardly belies the Spaniard's first description of it, and which may yet, if some confidence can but be established between the white and the black man, prove a valuable possession to the nation that undertakes the task of restoring order along its coasts.

The group consists of six large islands, each of which contains somewhere about 1500 to 2000 square miles, and twenty or thirty smaller ones; the whole forming a magnificent chain six hundred miles long. These islands attain high altitudes, probably at their highest some 8500 feet, and possess valuable physical advantages, such as broad sloping plains suitable for the growth of sugar and cotton, fine harbours, and sheltered channels and straits, and very probably, in the higher inland districts, considerable mineral wealth. One spot alone is there in their sunshine—a shadow, indeed, which one cannot but regard with infinite regret— and this is their climate. As far as we at present know, the climate is thoroughly and deplorably bad, and unless it is found that the higher elevations of the inland districts are less productive of fever to white men, this will no doubt form a serious drawback to all visions of European settlement or annexation by the Australian colonies. Of the natives I shall speak in the course of the next two or three chapters as occasion may arise: they are undoubtedly ingenious, and possessed of sterling qualities which only need directing into right channels. They build most admirable canoes, live in excellent houses, and are armed with weapons that would rank equally high whether considered as works of art or implements of aggression and defence.

Coming upon the group, as we did, from the westward, we first of all made the little off-lying island of Ulaua, situated between San Christoval, the most southern of the group, and Malanta. This island, like so many others that we had visited, was marvellously beautiful, but distinctly more Malayan in its vegetation than anything we had seen farther west or south, the trees being higher and the undergrowth if possible more prolific.

We landed on the lee side of the island, upon some sharp coral rocks, and were met by a hundred naked savages in a high state of pleasurable excitement. They took us at once by a rugged little path up the cliffs, and inland a few hundred yards, to their principal village, which was a long straggling place built in a clearing in the forest, having the appearance of an enormous avenue with tiny toy cottages scattered about at the foot of the trees. This clearing is perhaps a mile in length, and the houses are dotted here and there all the way along. They are better houses than we had been accustomed to, having sides four or five feet high and somewhat flat roofs; in fact, they resemble the poorer châlets of Switzerland. Everything, indeed, is different in this group of islands: the people are very distinctly Papuan, being much darker than the Santa Cruz or New Hebrides natives; both men and women, however, are splendidly formed, and in many cases very handsome. They wear no clothes here whatever, even the women not getting beyond a string round their waists. Their ornaments are more than usually various, and we noticed armlets and anklets formed of very prettily-arranged native beads, which were made from shells and dyed blue and red and yellow. Some of the girls wear a little mother-of-pearl bird, which is fixed into a hole in the extreme tip of the nose, and has a most singular appearance. These people are indeed very ingenious, and carve handsome bowls, which they inlay with mother-of-pearl and other shells; besides which, as I have said, they are noted canoe-makers.

Perhaps the Solomon Islands are more celebrated for their canoes than for anything else, and if so, I think with reason. Not even the gondolas of Venice are more exquisitely graceful than these little boats. They are made of bent planks of wood held together with strong thwarts and cemented with a kind of gum obtained from a tree. The stern is always carried up to a considerable height, like the bow of a gondola, and in large

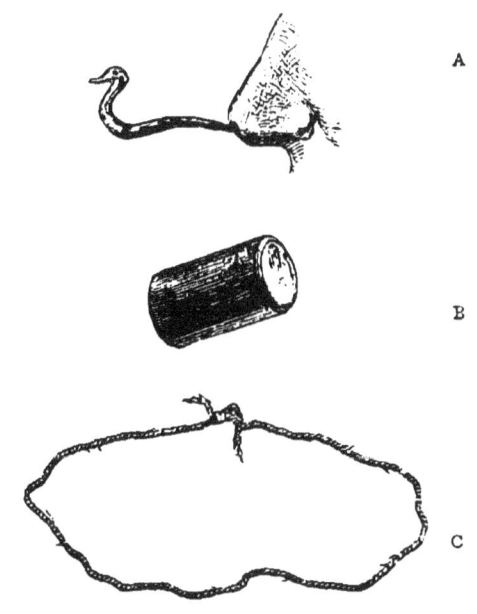

A LADY'S COSTUME, ULAUA, SOLOMON ISLANDS.

A, Mother-of-pearl ornament worn in the nose ; B, block worn through the ears ; C, waist string.

canoes both bow and stern are of the same graceful shape. They are narrow and have no outrigger, but sit on the water literally "like a duck." When the bow is not carried up in the gondola form I have mentioned, it is often made to represent a shark's head, and always in a canoe of any pretensions whatever there is a large amount of inlaying work, the designs being quaint and conventional, but certainly not without merit. I suppose these

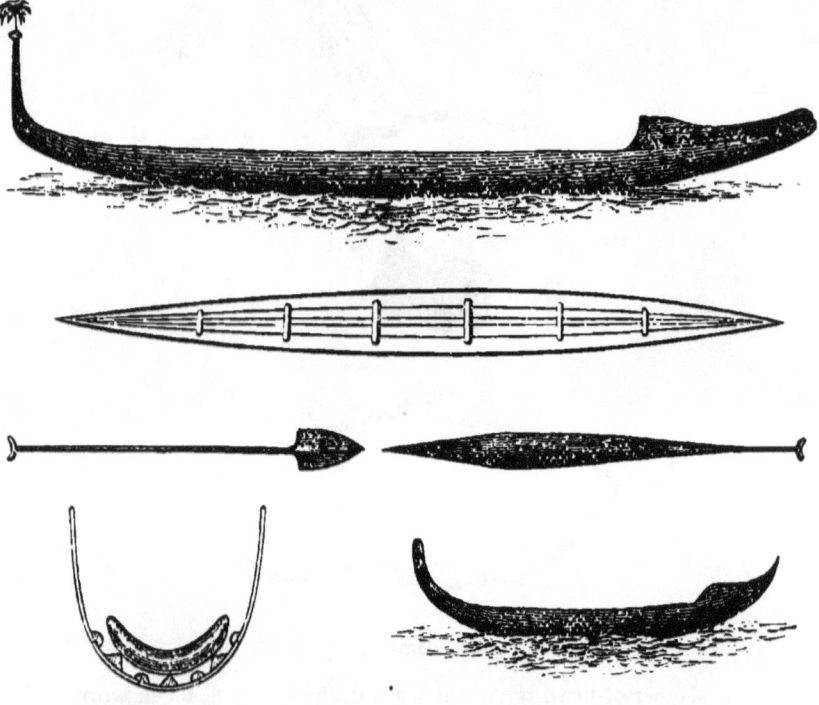

SOLOMON ISLAND CANOES.

canoes are the most "crank" craft in the world, yet the natives can take them out in fairly rough weather, and always manage them wonderfully. The paddles are short and thin, and are used indifferently on either side, two or three strokes on one side, then two or three on the other, and so on. In all the villages that we visited in this group we found one or two canoe-houses, where those not in use were kept, and almost every chief of note had a state canoe, usually in a house by itself. The work expended on some of the more magnificent ones surprised me very much, in some cases there being many thousands of pieces of pearl shell, all carefully shaped and let in in accordance with an elaborate design.

The Melanesian Mission has had a native teacher at Ulaua for some years, and it has been visited several times by the clergymen themselves. I was present at an examination of the natives, which was very amusing, the little naked urchins enjoying it all immensely, and exhibiting much pride when receiving any praise.

On our second visit to this place a month later we very nearly got into trouble, and as an example of the character of the natives I may as well mention what took place. A house had been built for the native teacher, which could be used as a school, and also as a sleeping-house when any of the missionaries wished to stay on the island. During the past year the chiefs of the village, thinking, I suppose, that the house was too good for its purpose, took partial possession and used it as a village club-house. When some objection was raised to this by the Bishop, the excuse was that an insufficient sum had been paid for the house in the first instance. An extra payment to the extent of a few axes and fish-hooks was accordingly determined upon, and the Bishop began handing these to the leading people. Upon giving one rather sullen-looking ruffian an axe he became intensely angry, and threw it upon the ground before us all in a great rage. This is always a sort of declaration of hostilities, and in a moment every one began shouting at once, angry words seemed to be passing, and none of us could make out what it was all about. The people were quite unarmed, or I fancy we might have got into some trouble here, for it seemed impossible to discover what was the matter, the native teacher being too excited or frightened to interpret properly. After a time, however, it appeared that some man of minor rank to the one who had thrown down the axe, had been given a present before his position entitled him to one, and his superior was in consequence highly indignant at the insult. The incident seemed to show me how easily a hostile feeling can be aroused amongst these people, and also how difficult it must be, unless one's knowledge of them is really very great, to avoid giving offence unintentionally.

We visited two or three places on the island of San Christoval, watering the ship at a charming little river on the northern end, and also calling at Wango, which in the old days, when whaling was more common, was often used as a watering-place.

The natives of this island have been utterly ruined by traders and whalers, and their condition now is really most pitiful. It is the old story : in Japan, in China, in Africa, in the Sandwich Islands, where you will, the white man seems for a long time only to change the vices of the natives. If he suppresses cannibalism, he introduces drunkenness. If he improves the laws of humanity, he makes more lax those of morality. I do not uphold the native *au naturel*—I mean the savage native ; I do not believe in the noble savage ; but I often feel that the difference between his wickedness and our wickedness is to a great extent one of kind. If we teach him not to kill, we teach him to cheat, which is the more wide-spreading and insidious crime of the two. If we are astonished at his neglect of mercy, he would often be no less astonished at our neglect of morality.

These Solomon Islanders have some fine traits and some honest healthy laws, for all their ferocity ; but to go to a place like this, and see how we have completely overthrown their better parts, and only partially substituted our wiser customs, is indeed a sad experience.*

* The Melanesian Mission has no station in this immediate district now ; the harm done by the traders is indeed so wide-spread and deeply rooted that, with his present staff and means, the Bishop considers it an almost hopeless task to attempt to grapple with the evil.

Wango is a large place, prettily situated on a river-bank; the houses are well-built, and in front have balconies, if one may call them so, like the huts of the New Zealand Maoris. The people themselves are handsome, the girls singularly, and I may add fatally, pretty; indeed, with the exception of the Sandwich Islanders, they are the best-looking natives I have seen. In most cases they wear no clothes, but are elaborately decorated with bangles, and I counted on one girl no less than twenty on each arm, all above the elbow. On the other bank of the river is another village, also of considerable size. Here I saw some really magnificent bowls, one in particular being over five feet long; they are conventionally designed to represent ducks, the bowl forming the body, an elaborately-wrought head and tail being added. In front of the duck's bill a fish is generally attached, and the whole is highly ornamented in mosaic fashion with pearl and other shells. The people are losing their art both in bowl-making and canoe-building, and we noticed in the village a ruined canoe-house, which in its day must have been a really fine building. The pillars are standing, each one being carved to represent sharks in the act of swallowing men. They are all different; in one the man going down head first, in another he is caught sitting, in a third the shark has him by the legs, and so on.

After leaving Wango we called at a place called Mwatta, which is less frequently visited perhaps, but here, too, the natives are utterly demoralised, and took no interest in us. The whalers and traders have done their work effectually, and the missionaries feel it impossible to make any stand against their influence. At this place when we went ashore no notice of us whatever was taken.

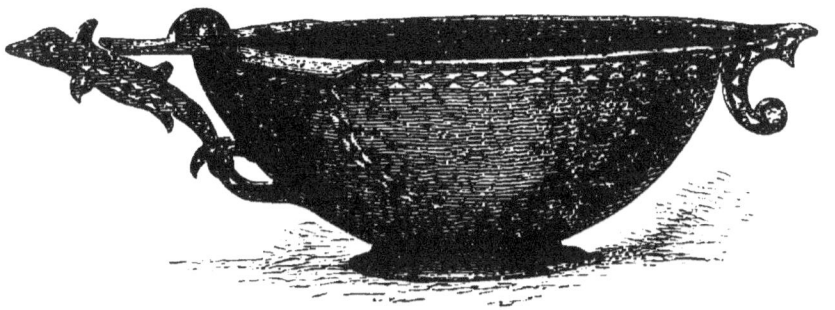

ORNAMENTED BOWL, WANGO, SOLOMON ISLANDS.

They seemed to know all about white people, and to want to have nothing to do with them. They are not, however, to any great extent emancipated from their old customs, if we may judge from the canoe-house, in which were hung twenty or thirty human skulls; one also was stuck outside, and the flesh was still upon it. The Bishop went and saw a sick man or two, and some sort of interest was shown in us after that; but the people seemed to be glad when we went down to the boat and pulled away.

CHAPTER X.

MALANTA AND FLORIDA.

THE next island we visited was Malanta, but we only called at two places; the most southerly one, Saä, being usually visited; the other, Pululaä, only having been called at once. The people of Malanta are undoubtedly most out-and-out ruffians. In the South Pacific Directory they are called "the most treacherous and blood-thirsty of any known savages," and I think with some truth.

We went ashore at Pululaä one morning, pulling into a small estuary round which mangroves were growing in great quantities. When we arrived at the mouth of the little river itself, we were somewhat surprised that no canoes came off, and that there were a great number of natives on the shore. On getting nearer in we noticed that these natives were all men, and all armed with an unusual number of long spears, and bows and arrows. Something was evidently about to take place, but what we could not tell. They did not shout nor show us any welcome; they merely drew themselves up in a line along the shore, their long spears standing up far above their heads, and having a most formidable appearance. There was no turning back now, however; so we pulled on until the boat grounded, and then jumped into the water and waded ashore. At first no one seemed to know us, nor could the Bishop remember any face amongst the wild crowd; but he kept repeating the chief's name, and so we waited for some time, hoping for a friendly face. These men were evi-

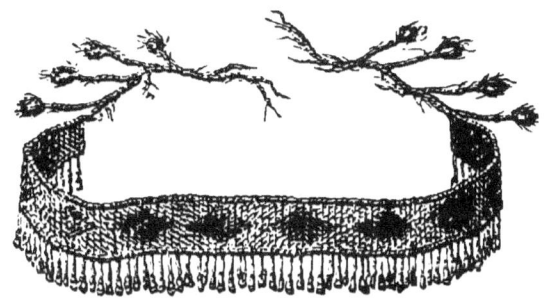

SOLOMON ISLAND SASH.

dently strangers, and did not know quite what attitude to assume. They made no actually hostile demonstration, but holding themselves aloof, shouted vociferously, and seemed to be ready for anything that might turn up. There were no women and children near, and this little army was far more elaborately equipped than is usual in ordinary times. Their ornaments in some cases were most beautiful; one or two men wearing wide sashes, as one might almost call them, of native bead-work, fringed

K

with human teeth. The more elaborate of these were worn over the right shoulder and round under the left arm. The colours were, as always in native workmanship, quiet and rich in tone and harmoniously arranged.

After a rather awkward delay of twenty minutes or so, during which we laughed and talked amongst ourselves, and endeavoured to appear quite at our ease, a merry old fellow arrived, who turned out to be the chief whom the Bishop had seen on his former visit. This man spoke a few words to the crowd, evidently assuring them that he knew who we were, after which they were willing to trade in bows and arrows and spears and ornaments. This old chief had been kidnapped when a boy and taken to Fiji, where he had worked for several years, and had learned a few of the more common English oaths, with which he now besprinkled his conversation. His son was sick, and he succeeded in making the Bishop understand that he should like him to be doctored. We also made out with some difficulty that the assembling of these armed ruffians was on account of a feast to be given that night at the village; natives from far and wide had been invited, and were coming in all day long from the neighbourhood. The customs at these feasts are very curious. No part of the food provided, for instance, is *eaten* at the entertainment. Each guest, on the contrary, brings such provisions as are necessary for his own use during his stay, and takes his share of the feast away with him when he goes. Our idea of "eat what you can, but pocket none," is exactly reversed, and "pocket what you can, but eat none," is the Solomon Island practice. This custom is necessitated by the "taboo" laws, which are so severe in this group that at a public feast it would be almost impossible to avoid some infringement of these complicated regulations; the difficulty is therefore avoided by the food being taken away and eaten at home. Without attempting any entrance upon so wide a field as the question of tabooing, I may illustrate the sort of complications that arise when the food is eaten on the spot by a single example. If after a meal a visitor should purposely or accidentally retain a morsel of the food, he is enabled thereby to exercise a mysterious influence over the giver of the feast. The host considering himself thus charmed, will redeem the lost fragment at as high a figure as he can afford. A piece of betel-nut was, at a feast on a neighbouring island, carried away by a guest a few weeks previous to our visit. The chief fell ill, and imagined something was wrong; at length he discovered what had taken place, and although the man with the piece of betel-nut was living far away upon another island, sent across to him, and redeemed the fragment for forty dog's teeth, which is an equivalent for four thousand coco-nuts!

While doing a brisk trade in ornaments and spears with the rough crowd on shore, I bought a bow and a bundle of arrows from one ill-looking native for a good-sized knife. He seemed very eager to close the bargain, and I was no less anxious, for both bow and arrows were very fine of their kind. When I handed him the knife, however, he slipped the arrows into my hand and disappeared through the crowd with my bow! One can do nothing on such an occasion, for it is obviously unwise to initiate a disturbance. On the other hand, if the natives imagine you can be quite easily cheated, their opinion of you does not remain very high. As a rule, in such cases all trading is stopped until the stolen article is returned, but in this instance, there being so many strangers present and their whole aspect being so far from reassuring, we deemed discretion the better part of valour.

ORNAMENT WORN ON FOREHEAD.
Tortoise-shell fretwork upon a shell disc; about ⅙ actual size.

I have said nothing of the spears used by the natives of the Solomon Islands. They are certainly the finest weapons in the South Seas, and I secured one that was as much as sixteen feet long, a single black shaft, highly polished and ornamented at the "business end" with an elaboration of human bone and coloured fancy binding that defies all description. The spears more usually carried are about ten feet long, and also made of black polished wood, and tipped with human bone. There are, near the extremity of these weapons, ten or a dozen barbs resembling the tip of the spear, which are fastened to the shaft by a binding of coloured cane-work, the whole being held together and strengthened with the same resinous substance as used in canoe-building. The price of such spears as the ones I have last mentioned is from one stick to a stick and a half of tobacco, equivalent to about three-halfpence.

Leaving these people to their evening feast—and let us hope there was to be nothing on the *menu* worse than pigs' flesh and yams—we sailed down the so-called Indispensable Strait to the little group of islands known as the Floridas.

Indispensable Strait lies between the two long and mountainous islands of Malanta and Guadalcanar. The Floridas close it at the north-west, and the island of San Christoval at the south-east end. It is accordingly almost land-locked, and about a hundred and fifty miles long by forty broad. The mountains of Guadalcanar are as much as eight thousand feet high, and of exceedingly picturesque outline. Whilst sailing amongst the islets of the little Florida group we did experience the typical and usually-accepted enjoyments of South Sea Island cruising. The weather was, at least for a day or two, almost perfect—the sea blue, the islands green, the waves upon the reefs like snowy foam. Behind this foreground were the great purple mountain-peaks of Guadalcanar, curiously fascinating to us on account of their never having been visited by white men or black. The poor superstitious natives report the existence of hairy men and giant crocodiles, and I know not what terrors beside; but even the so-called hill tribes have not probably explored beyond the more accessible passes, and there is every reason to believe the higher country is quite uninhabited. Between the mountains and the sea on Guadalcanar is some fine-looking flat country, which resembles in appearance that of the Rewa district in Fiji, and will doubtless some day grow sugar and cotton for the markets of Europe.

We went ashore to shoot pigeons one day upon a little uninhabited island in the Straits. It was well-wooded and very beautiful. Remains of huts were found upon the shore, as though some fishing parties had temporarily lived there. I also found a native oven of smooth round stone, and by it a human skull and a few loose bones: the story of that poor creature's death needs no telling.

The Florida group, lying at the upper end of

this Indispensable Strait, is but little known, and is set down on the Admiralty charts with the wildest inaccuracy. We slept ashore one night at Gaeta, upon the most southern island of the little archipelago. The place had been literally rescued from heathenism by Mr. Penny, of the Melanesian Mission, within the last two years. The village at which we stopped was a few miles from the shore and in a high and picturesque situation: we struggled up to it along the swampy forest path, escorted by twenty or thirty natives, on a beautiful and quiet evening in August. Near the village, through a steep ravine, ran a fairly broad stream, in which we had a pleasant bath—no ordinary luxury in these South Sea Islands. The houses in this district are mostly of the kind known as "platform houses"; they are, that is to say, elevated some four feet from the ground, and have a balcony in front upon which one can sit and enjoy the fresh air and lovely view to one's heart's content. I enjoyed my evening here more than any other during my cruise. The natives were kind and cheerful, we were all in good spirits, and the air was cool and even invigorating. Whilst I sat upon the balcony the Bishop held a service in the house, and gave, through an interpreter, a short address. I suppose there were over fifty natives crowded into the little room, and a curious congregation indeed they were. Old white-haired warriors, with strange thoughts, doubtless, concerning these new times, so different from the days of their youth and manhood ; scraggy old hags, with shrunken breasts and careworn look, crouching in corners with grim attention ; finely-made, healthful Florida beauties, with bright eyes and clever faces— upon their arms some, doubtless to them, coquettish

PLATFORM HOUSES, SOLOMON ISLANDS.

ornament, and round their waists an ample fringe, which stood out in a droll manner like a ballet girl's skirt; young lusty warriors, too, in the prime of their youth, who laid their bows and spears outside the door, and listened quietly to the strange news the mighty white man had to tell. Lastly, and these in greatest numbers, stowed away amongst the rest and covering the matted floor so thickly as not to leave a foot of space, the invariable, quaint, old-fashioned little boys and girls—always the same, their bullet heads so loosely fixed on, their long thin limbs, their bright and gleaming eyes, their funny playful ways, so pretty, and yet one cannot help feeling so painfully monkey-like. Negro or Indian, or Arab or Malay, how alike they are—as everywhere, so too not a whit different here in Melanesia. I sat outside listening to the little songs they sang, and watching the fireflies flitting to and fro among the trees, and the great sago palms looming weirdly overhead, and the dark hill beyond, above which the evening star was setting—nothing could have been more quiet, solemn, peaceful.

This house, in which we slept, has an uncomfortable notoriety, which I confess during the night dispelled much of the romance of our situation. It is the resort from time to time of divers predatory centipedes, which in this island are conspicuous for both ferocity and appetite. I believe their bite is not fatal, but it is sufficiently serious to make even the natives as frightened of them as of alligators. "Always there is a black spot in our sunshine "— in these tropic climes snakes, alligators, mosquitoes, sharks, centipedes ! Truly Nature gives us no rose without its thorn. For my part, centipedes were simply feeding on me the night through, and the few occasions when we had a scare and lit a candle were the only moments of relief! *

Savo is a pretty island of this group, and we called there upon two occasions. I had looked forward to this place with great interest as the chief had been on board with us ever since leaving Norfolk Island.

This Lord of Savo—as an Eastern dragoman would say (*vide* Kinglake), this Scorner of the Solomons and Suppressor of Florida—had quitted his government, and left his enemies to breathe for a moment, and had crossed the waters in the strict disguise of a shirt and pair of trousers, with a small but eternally faithful retinue of followers, in order that he might look upon the overpowering magnificence of the Melanesian Mission head-quarters! He was a friendly and good-natured old fellow, and we had spent many hours together trying to exchange ideas in the usual pantomimic manner. I had, moreover, corrupted him by

* Eight weeks after our visit to Gaeta the terrible massacre of Lieutenant-Commander Bower, of H.M.S. *Sandfly*, and four seamen, occurred. The actual site of the attack was a small uninhabited island, off which our vessel lay during the inland excursion described above. It is somewhat remarkable that this place, where we were so cordially welcomed, and where I spent my only night on shore during the entire cruise, should in such a short time become so fatally notorious. Some further particulars and comments upon this massacre will be found in Chapter XIV.

countless donations of tobacco and other treasures, in return for which I was given to understand that when I set foot upon the land of his inheritance I should be overwhelmed by hospitality and curiosities. How was my faith in the nobility of the savage chief overthrown when, at the end of my second visit, I became aware that the only return I had received for my generosity consisted in a well-rifled bunch of very inferior bananas; I even found myself bargaining hotly with one of this nobleman's retinue for a spear just as we were leaving, and in desperation, by the assistance of an interpreter, pleaded that he, the chief, would intercede on my behalf. He was equal to the occasion. "It's not my spear," he cried with feeling; "if it were mine I'd *give* it to you : I could'nt sell you anything. It belongs to the people on shore!" I left Savo with an entirely new opinion concerning the nobility of Melanesian chieftains!

CHAPTER XI.

YSABEL.

THERE was nothing of special interest in the other places we visited in the Floridas. Here was a fine harbour; here the *Dancing Wave* was cut out several years ago; here a man-of-war punished the natives for some atrocity or other: such were the distinguishing marks of most of our places of call. After a few days' cruising in and out amongst the intricacies of the group, we steered northwards once more, and were shortly at anchor in the very beautiful harbour of Santa Ysabel de la Estrella, as Mendaña called it three hundred years ago. Here is a pretty little anchorage within a great gulf, known on some charts as "Thousand Ships Bay." The native name of the district is Bugotu, and it being the Ultima Thule of our cruise, we lay here several days.

The curse of the northern Solomon Islands is an institution known as "head-hunting." The more savage tribes make collections of heads with which to adorn their houses, and are as assiduous in their search for these articles of vertu as any collector in

Europe is for old china. The mere acquisition of such old heads among their own people as may turn up in the natural course of things, does not satisfy these zealous hunters. They go far afield for their highly-prized ornaments, and organise extensive expeditions, sweeping down on weaker tribes and carrying off all they can seize. The southern end of the island of Ysabel is a favourite hunting-ground for the more northern tribes, who come down in great force, bringing large canoes full of warriors from the islands of Choiseul and New Georgia. The more peaceful southerners make no attempt at resistance, but have built themselves strongholds into which they retire and if possible defy their enemies. These places of refuge are of two kinds —tree houses and hill fortifications. The tree houses possess the greatest interest, and in some parts of the island are quite numerous and even used as ordinary places of residence in times of peace. The people attain almost the agility of monkeys by continually climbing up and down these trees and walking along their branches.

At the village near which we first anchored there was but one tree house, but it was very good of its kind. The tree in which it was built was a magnificent one growing upon the cliff by the shore; all the lower branches were cleared away, and its peculiar appearance made it most conspicuous amongst the surrounding palms and smaller growth.

There was a cleared space around the foot of this giant, and from the branches hung a slender rattan-cane ladder. The ascent is certainly not a very enjoyable affair; the ladder seems of the very weakest, and swings about unpleasantly; the rounds, moreover, are merely bits of stick lashed on to a single cane rope, and afford practically no foothold to the booted European. On reaching the top I was surprised to find a large well-built house, quite level, and fixed in among the branches with the greatest ingenuity. The floor is covered with mats and scrupulously clean. It is twenty-six feet long by eighteen wide, and the ridge-pole is ten feet from the floor. The strength and solidity of the whole structure is most remarkable, and I suppose at a pinch nearly all the inhabitants of the village might find refuge here. At either end of this house are pleasant balconies, one of which seemed literally to overhang the sea, which lay more than a hundred feet beneath. The height of the house from the ground is between seventy and eighty feet. Arrayed along the sides are numbers of small heaps of stones for defensive purposes. When a raid by the head-hunters is reported, the people all retire to this curious fortress, and drawing the thin ladder up after them, they can defy their enemies. If the invaders come near to try and cut down the tree (no light work, for the trunk is hard as iron), the besieged party pelt them with stones from above;

TREE HOUSE, YSABEL, SOLOMON ISLANDS.

and unless the enemy were armed with rifles, I should say these tree fortresses were quite impregnable. Other fortresses there are upon this island, as I have said, and these are but little less curious; they are perched upon bold rocky peaks, and the approaches are in some cases cut off by the construction of large dykes or fosses, upon which a most surprising amount of labour must at one time have been expended.

I enjoyed the few days we spent amongst these people immensely; they are certainly ingenious in their various arts. The houses are quite models of workmanship, neat, prim, and clean, and are all of the platform kind, which in so damp a climate is almost a necessity.

Some of the canoes belonging to the village were more magnificent than any I have seen, one in particular being simply covered with shells and decorations of all sorts; they are kept more for show than use, however, and are the pride of the chief and the envy of all visitors. I am afraid the people here are, notwithstanding their ingenuity, far from industrious, for they possess but few weapons and make native cloth only in small quantities; their yam plantations are by no means admirable; and their chief delight seems to be in sitting on their hams upon the shore, with their shields and tomahawks beside them, gazing vacantly into space.

Traders call frequently, and almost every man

YSABEL.

has an axe mounted upon a black wood handle of his own manufacture. The name of this weapon is "mattiana," which signifies "his death," and the possession of one is every young Bugotu man's ambition. In the evenings the more enterprising men will do a little fishing, perching themselves upon high tripods which are erected on shallow

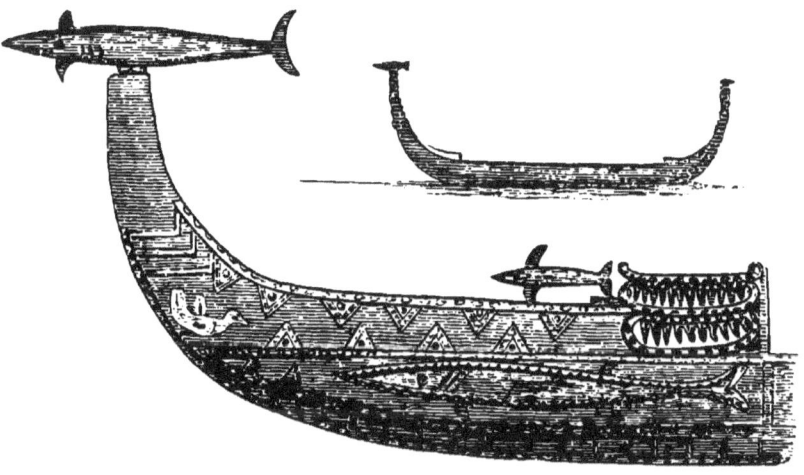

SOLOMON ISLAND STATE CANOE.

patches near the shore, and working a large net between four of them. The island abounds in cockatoos, toucans, and both green and scarlet parrots. Whilst bathing in the little stream one morning, the cockatoos became so enraged at our intrusion, and withal so curious to know more of who or what we were, that they assembled round us in scores, screaming with anger, and we could have knocked them down with sticks: it was a most amusing experience.

The money used in the Solomon Islands is interesting, and I am tempted to give a rather detailed account of it. The general currency, consisting of strings of shell beads about the size of shirt buttons, very well made, and strung in fathom lengths, is of two kinds, known as red money and white money. Above this in the scale of value come dogs' teeth, which are the gold of this coinage. Only two teeth from a dog's jaw can be used as legal tender, and their value is very considerable, as will be seen from the table I give below. A hole is drilled in each tooth, and when a man has a sufficient number, he sets them on a band of suitable width and wears them as a collar; I have seen a collar of this kind which would be worth perhaps not less than £20 of our money. Porpoise teeth are also used, but are only one-fifth as valuable as dogs' teeth. One other coin obtains, which seems to be a ring of *marble:* it is worn upon the chest, and is looked upon as a charm as well as a legitimate coin. The value of these different moneys varies but little throughout the group, and may be roughly estimated as follows:—

10 coco-nuts = 1 string of white money, or 1 flat stick of tobacco.
10 strings white money = 1 string red money, or 1 dog's tooth.

10 strings red money	= 1 "isa," or 50 porpoise teeth.
10 isas	= 1 good-quality wife.
1 "bakiha" (marble ring)	= 1 head among the head-hunters.
1 bakiha	= 1 very good pig.
1 bakiha	= 1 medium young man.

From this table it will be seen that a wife such as would be considered a suitable match for any rising young islander is worth about ten thousand coco-nuts. This price is of course a very variable one, depending, however, far more upon the social position of the father than upon the good looks or qualities of the girl herself.

The customs in connection with marriages possess something of interest. When a man proposes for the hand of a girl he strikes a bargain with the father, who of course rates his property as highly as possible—say at ten thousand coco-nuts. This the wild aspirant is perhaps unable to pay; but he goes round to his friends, and in consideration of so much work to be done when required, succeeds in borrowing from them the necessary sum. The girl is then engaged, and an indefinite time elapses before things are brought to a conclusion. At the marriage a feast is given, and the relatives and friends who advanced money to the bridegroom are of course asked. To these, presents are made in proportion to the magnitude of the loans. For instance, uncle A., who gave two white strings, gets fifty yams; friend C., who gave some dogs' teeth, gets a pig; and so on; the amount thus returned being about fifty per cent. of the original donation.

Not an unnatural consequence of this custom arises, and that is, the men who put too high a value upon their daughters do not get them married.

Takua, a great Florida chief, has three daughters, all unmarried. One rash wight had, the year previous to my visit, proposed for the youngest, but discovered that her price was sixty thousand coco-nuts! The man struggled to raise the sum, but failed. Then the chief Takua rose up in his wrath and fined him a thousand coco-nuts for daring to propose when he had not the necessary wealth. The poor fellow employed a professional pleader to try and obtain a reversion of this sentence, but he lost his case, and has been a disgraced man ever since.

These Solomon Island beauties are by no means to be thought lightly of; they are short but well-made girls, with pretty hands and feet. Their faces are covered with a very delicate tattooing, which is colourless, and only visible when seen quite closely. The process, an important event in every girl's life, is somewhat thus: A number of people are hired (for a porpoise tooth apiece) to sing and howl for a whole night round the girl's house, thus keeping her from sleep. The next day the artist arrives—his pay is high, often many thousands of coco-nuts (or of course their equivalent), and the operation is proceeded with. A pattern is carved all over the face, and consists of a number of sets of concentric circles or polygons, the outer ones of which are about the size of a sixpence; the entire design resembles cells of a honeycomb. When the operation is completed, the girl, overtired from pain and want of sleep, is left to rest for many hours, at the end of which time the smarting will have considerably diminished.

After a few comparatively uneventful calls at various points on the islands of Malanta and San Christoval, we started away from the Solomons, laying a south-easterly course towards the Torres Islands. For *thirteen* miserable days we beat against a strong south-east trade-wind, making in all that time only 360 miles, and experiencing terrific squalls, at the rate sometimes of thirty or forty a day. Any one who wants to know how uncomfortable a sailing vessel can be, should try a fortnight's beating under double-reefed topsails against fresh gales in a hundred-ton vessel. At times the motion for hours together was so violent that we could neither sit nor lie without holding on. Before we started upon our actual course from

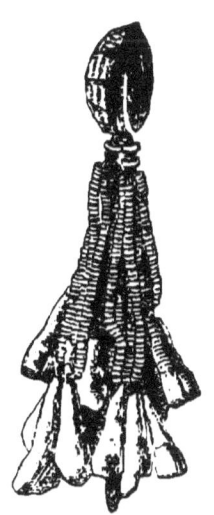

EAR PENDANT.
Inlaid black wood, native bead-work, and human teeth.

the one group of islands to the other we had had bad weather, and it lasted until we were down to the south of the New Hebrides; so that in reality our ill-fortune in the matter of wind and waves continued for fully a month. During that time we had no relief for even so much as a few consecutive hours. Twice we were obliged to lay to; the ship the whole time was drenched from stem to stern; everything below was damp and mouldy; the crew were sick, the natives were sick, and we ourselves were bilious and cross. It was now almost three months since we had tasted fresh meat or other vegetables than yams, and even bread was almost an unknown luxury; we felt that we had some right therefore to grumble at this additional burden of adverse weather. I must not, however, forget to add that our little vessel behaved through it all most admirably. I felt there was no limit to her endurance; we had only to trim two little sails and lash the wheel, and there she would have ridden for a month if need had been. Whilst struggling to reach the Torres Islands it is true that our forestay was disabled, but it only necessitated some six or seven hours' delay; and I may here state as a somewhat wonderful fact, and certainly an encouraging one to timid landsmen, that although I have travelled by sea a distance of over a hundred thousand miles, this seven hours' halt for repairs upon the little sailing vessel *Southern Cross* was the longest detention on account of a mishap that I have experienced.

At the end of the fourth week of head winds we obtained a slant from the eastward, and so, having held on for as much as two hundred and fifty miles out of our course, in hope of such a change, we were at last able to bear down without any further tacking to the Loyalty Islands.

CHAPTER XII.

THE LOYALTY ISLANDS.

ON the tenth of September I was put down on Nengone, in the Loyalty group, and the *Southern Cross* proceeded on her way south to Norfolk Island. I felt more sorry than I had thought possible to leave the little vessel on which I had spent three months, seeing so much that was new and strange. I had made many friends amongst our native passengers, who, notwithstanding the barbarity of their early surroundings, were in the main a good-hearted merry lot.

From Nengone I hoped to find some means of crossing to Noumea, in New Caledonia, from which port a steamer runs fortnightly to Sydney. Mr. and Mrs. Jones, of the London Missionary Society, received me with great kindness, and made me much at home during the few days I spent with them. They were quiet, restful days, after cruising for so long in the little Mission vessel during, for the most part, not too peaceful weather. Mr. Jones has a large house and all such surroundings and conveniences as one sees on an Australian station; he has been on the Island for twenty-five years, and I may add is one of the most popular alike among missionaries, traders, and adventurers, of all the white men in the South Seas.

There had been a "war" on the island since we called on our way north, and the excitement consequent upon this state of things was as intense as it was natural. The decisive battle was fought only a few days before I landed, and twenty-one persons were killed, eleven of whom, however, I regret to say, were children! It was a battle of revenge for injuries received by the Protestants at the hands of their Roman Catholic neighbours.

The French took possession of this island, more or less formally, in 1866, their hold upon it previous to that being merely nominal. Shortly after the introduction of a Resident, certain Roman Catholic priests were sent to convert the natives, and these, I need hardly add, did not co-operate very amicably with the Protestant missionary. From that time, indeed, to this, a feeling of hostility has existed between the Romanist converts and the Protestants. On several occasions outbreaks have occurred, one of which was so serious that it resulted in the removal of the Catholics and their entire flock to the Isle of Pines.

The feeling is now hostile beyond all mending. How strange it seems that a people but now rescued from cannibalism (it is not ten years ago that a boy was eaten at this very village where I stayed), with hardly a conception of Christ other than that, instead of being a great warrior chief, He was the Prince of Peace, should have their very worst passions aroused in a religious contest! The whole island is torn up with the passion of this quarrel. It burns in their breasts as no heathen feud has ever burned. It cannot be laid aside. The very boys and children are interested, and their hatred of the rival creed knows no limit. This state of things appeared to me the more sad because in all other respects I found here a model community. The people, apart from this disastrous quarrel, seem more benefited by missionary work than any I have seen. Their enthusiasm in religious matters is most remarkable. They have built themselves a large and handsome church; they buy dresses and European costumes, in which, however, they look entirely hideous, as all savages in civilised habiliments do; they give five or six hundred a year to their missionary society, and are in very many respects models of generosity and religious zeal. Through all the South Seas, moreover, no men are more noted for bravery than those of this group; so that if there is any reckless expedition or voyage of discovery on hand, the promoter always endeavours to obtain a Loyalty Island crew.

I cannot say I think the French rule here is other than pernicious, their policy being one of interference and aggression. Seeing that the natives are quiet and well-behaved enough, the motto of their political governors should be "Ça ira"; instead of which the authorities take the exactly opposite course, and are continually meddling where interference is inexpedient and even fatal. These people have their own hereditary chiefs and native customs, but the French come in, set up other chiefs of their own creation, and make laws that violate the traditional habits of the islanders. The result, as can only be expected, is continual ill-feeling, insubordination, and even rebellion.*

I spent five very pleasant days with Mr. Jones, the missionary, and found his people were models of kindness and good manners. He had brought up the men to many useful trades, so that one could build, another do joinery, a third make boats. The women were no less useful, waiting neatly and well

---

* The French are here most cordially hated by the natives; they are not even admitted to be white men. Such conversations as this I have held with the more educated, who speak a little English :—

"What feller that boat belong? He belong white man?"

" No, he no belong white man."

" What feller he belong, then ? "

" Oh, he belong oui-oui man."

" Well, then, he belong *white* man?"

" Oh, no ; oui-oui man no belong white man ; oui-oui man belong all same devil." (I need hardly say "oui-oui man" is sandlewood English for Frenchman.)

at table, keeping the house clean and in good order, milking the cows, making butter, cooking, and the like.

There are two traders on the island, who collect from the natives such fungus, copra, &c., as they may have, and give them in exchange tobacco, calicoes, and so on. One of these men had built himself a small cutter of about six tons burden, in which I arranged to go to Noumea. I rode across the island to the bay where we had landed from the *Southern Cross* some months before, and embarked on my tiny vessel at sunset on a lovely evening. We had three natives to help in working the little cutter, the owner and myself occupying the toy cabin aft. There was a heavy sea in the passage between the Loyalty group and New Caledonia, but not much wind; the result was, we knocked about in a manner that was positively awful. When daylight broke in the morning we were out of sight of land, and in a very unsatisfactory position. For the greater part of the day we tossed listlessly about on the open sea, but a wind springing up in the afternoon, we made the high land, and steered up towards the entrance known as Havannah Passage. The tide running through this pass was very strong, and as it met the easterly wind, formed a curious sea resembling a whirlpool, to which I remember having seen nothing similar, unless it were the Niagara river below the falls.

To steer in between this curiously-broken water and the raging breakers on the reef required no small amount of skill, and once or twice it seemed as though one of the great waves would surely break on the weather side of us, in which case it would have been all over with ourselves as well as the cutter, for no one could hope to live amongst such breakers.

The reefs of New Caledonia, like those of Fiji, are very extensive, and run out many miles from the shore, forming beautiful lagoons, inside which even large steamers may sail, but also constituting a considerable source of danger in these seas, where the charts are far from accurate.

We ran for fifty miles round the south-east end of New Caledonia, amongst small islands and under great headlands that reminded me of the coast of Greece; it was a lovely sail in the bright light of the full moon, and although the mountains were gaunt and barren in reality, their appearance that night was very beautiful.

New Caledonia is the largest of the so-called South Sea Islands, being, independent of the Isle of Pines and outlying reefs, as much as two hundred and thirty miles long and between thirty and forty broad. A range of mountains runs along the entire length of the island, leaving but a narrow margin of useful land on each side. This will always prove a great hindrance to any opening up or extensive development of the country. Internal communication will be but indifferent for many years to come, and it may be doubted if the island will ever become of great value, unless its mineral resources turn out to be what some sanguine New Caledonians predict. It has most certainly the appearance of a mineral country. There are indications of iron upon every hillside, the mountains presenting much brilliant colouring. We passed close under Mont d'Or, a very fine headland, supposedly rich in nickel and other metals, but whose title is a misnomer. Late at night we pulled into Noumea harbour; the wind had entirely dropped, the moon was full, and the water like a mirror, as we rowed slowly in through the shipping.

I had expected to find the mail steamer from Sydney lying in Noumea, as her day of sailing was the following one. Passing under the stern of a small schooner, I accordingly shouted to a native who was leaning against the bulwarks, " Steamer, he no come ? "

" No," was his answer; "steamer he no come—steamer he stop on a stone—all man he go salt water—plenty man he die—steamer he finish."

This was serious news indeed, and it seemed true enough, for we found the French man-of-war getting up steam, and making all haste to start in search of the missing packet.

I went to bed at once, being tired out, and

determined to leave the question of the steamer's non-appearance until the morrow. The alarm proved a false one, as appeared the next day, the vessel's departure from Sydney having been delayed forty-eight hours by the San Francisco mail, with which this one runs in connection.

CHAPTER XIII.

NEW CALEDONIA.

NOUMEA, capital of New Caledonia and its dependencies, is a hot, dusty, squarely-planned town; the streets, broad and straight and shadeless; the houses, low and wooden, with corrugated iron roofs. Billiard-saloons and drinking-bars seem more general than shops, and billiard-playing and drinking seem more popular pursuits than working. There are no trees in the streets; there is nothing pleasant to look upon wherever you may turn. There is nothing Frenchlike beyond the long thin lettering of the shop-signs—I do not speak of the people, I speak merely of Noumea. It is twin sister to Port Said, than which I suppose one could say nothing less flattering.

Noumea, blinking in the sunlight—Noumea, sunburnt, scorched, dried up—great heaven! what a place for light-hearted Frenchmen to come to! And yet they are here, surely enough. At the bars drinking syrups, and in the saloons playing billiards, and at their little shop-doors, here they indeed are, with low-cut waistcoats, and narrow black ties, and sallow, moustachioed faces. The women too, tripping up the street or sitting in their shops, are no less unmistakable—so daintily shod, so neatly dressed, with such good figures and bewitching airs. They all seemed out of place though, men and women too, with their bowing and shoulder-shrugging and hat-raising and energetic conversing ; the tropical sun and the shadeless, long, unlovely streets seemed unsuited to them.

Busy English merchants are to be seen also in Noumea in fair numbers, and lazy sea captains, such as are never seen on shore more than a mile away from wharfs and landings, and who have about them a general feeling (in the sense in which a modern upholsterer talks about a cabinet with a Chippendale " feeling ") of oakum and Stockholm tar. More noticeable, however, than any other class of people are the convicts, who are to be seen in considerable numbers everywhere. Those that walk freely about the streets are " libérés," or, as we should call them, "ticket-of-leave men." Others, also at liberty in the streets, are exiles serving a term of banishment. Here are even stately Arabs in fez and turban and long white skirts—political offenders from Algiers. Lastly, I must notice the gangs of hard-labour convicts passing through the streets to their work with armed escort.

There are now about eight thousand prisoners in New Caledonia, the great majority of whom are quartered on the island of Nou, which lies within the harbour, and upon which are large prisons, barracks, workshops, &c. &c. One or two smaller prison stations are situated on the main island, but these are of but little importance compared with the establishment at Nou. A ticket-of-leave system is in force, land being given in a way which I find rather obscurely described as "conditionellement et dans une proportion raisonnable." These libérés now amount to about two thousand; they form small settlements amongst themselves, and mix but little with the immigrants.

To free settlers this French colony does not apparently present any attraction, some few hundreds, at an outside estimate, constituting the annual immigration from France. The fact is, New Caledonia has not succeeded in becoming much more than a penal settlement. All the people in Noumea are Government people; all the talk is of appointments and promotions, and of prospects of being removed to Réunion or to Saigon. Frenchmen in New Caledonia do not ever look upon the place as a home; they do not even look upon it as an adopted home. The spirit here is similar to that of the military community at Aden, or some similar station. Whether or not it was owing to my recent visits to Australia and New Zealand, and the consequent strength of contrast, I do not know, but when in New

Caledonia I felt more than ever the truth of the assertion, that Frenchmen will never make good colonists.

I had a long and interesting drive one afternoon in the country. The roads are magnificent, being the result of convict labour. Passing the outskirts of the little town (Noumea has only three thousand inhabitants), where are barracks and "departments" without end, and villas that are not pretty or attractive, but *mean* in appearance, we get out into the country, or, as all English-speaking people call it, the "bush." They may well call it bush, for what do I see? Surely not; yet—yes it *is*—the old universal, everlasting, omnipresent, never-green gum, the same stunted, white-barked, shaggy, gnarled, ugly eucalyptus that one sees everywhere in Australia from Cape York to King George's Sound. This New Caledonia, then, belongs evidently to the Australian continent, and not to the South Sea Islands.

The immediate country is as like that around Adelaide as anything could well be, but the high finely-shaped mountains they have not on the Australian mainland. We passed a few native houses with fool's-cap-like roofs reaching to a great height; there are not many natives round Noumea, however, as since the late insurrection they have been driven far back into the mountain districts. It is supposed that there are still between twenty

NATIVE HOUSE, NEW CALEDONIA.

and thirty thousand in New Caledonia, but that they have decreased over fifty per cent. during the last half-century. The only thing of special interest that occurs to me in connection with them is, that they adopt the same extraordinary costume, if one can call it so, as that worn by some of the tribes of South Africa.

It was cool and pleasant as we rattled back through the now almost deserted streets ; but more pleasant still was it when, an hour or so afterwards, I found myself—after a more than three months' entire ignorance of such things—seated at a prettily-set table, with ladies passably fair and gentlemen presumably brave, discussing dinner in a cool, open room, whilst native servants glided noiselessly about—everything so comfortable, so pleasant, so luxurious.

The business of Noumea is practically all in English hands. The shipping, although obliged to sail under French colours, is also English. The steamers on the coast are English. The mail contract with Sydney (£6000 a year) is with an English company. What is French is only the administration, the red-tapeism, and the management of the convicts.

I was sorry not to be able to see the northern part of the island, which indeed would justify more eulogies than I am able to pass upon the Noumea district. It is no doubt a rich country in places, and capable of growing sugar to some extent, although I firmly believe the mineral interest is the only one to which one can reasonably look for any great amount of success.

    I sailed for Sydney on a Sunday morning, nearly all the Europeans in the settlement, consisting of not an inconsiderable number of well-dressed ladies, and perhaps a hundred idle lookers-on, assembling upon the quay to see the steamer away. We were two hours steaming across the wide lagoon, then past the lighthouse, and out through the reef. It is perhaps the last South Sea Island reef I shall ever see, and I watched it with great interest, stretching away as far as eye could reach to right and left. The old, now so familiar sound, the well-known, ever-beautiful, tumbling, snowy surf—I was indeed sorry to see the last of it.

CHAPTER XIV.

LABOUR AND TRADE IN THE WESTERN PACIFIC.

OF the labour traffic carried on so largely between the islands and Queensland, Fiji and New Caledonia, I may perhaps say a few words now. I do not wish to make invidious comparisons between these three centres of labour importation. I will merely say that in my own opinion the abuses are greatest in New Caledonia, for the reason that the French Government has not taken even so much as the insignificant interest in the subject that our own authorities have indulged in. The labour trade is in a bad state everywhere, whether under French flag or English, and what is said here on the subject applies equally to all the colonies to which natives are taken. The question is a very difficult one to approach, chiefly because the moment any one attempts to point to the abuses that take place, he is put down as belonging to the sentimental and so-called "Exeter Hall" party, with whom truly one cannot have much patience. For my own part, I believe that we, as a civilised nation, have no right to hire native men until we have first made them clearly understand what our terms of engagement are. At present the labour trade is merely a disguised slave trade. It is said the islanders are paid. Yes, but what does the pay amount to? Even if the "trade" given as wages were honest stuff, it would be no payment to them. They give it all away as soon as they land at their homes, and have not, nor can possibly have, any conceivable use for it. I have myself seen quite new corduroy trousers, the value of which must have been nearly a sovereign, sold back to white men for a few pence worth of tobacco. I have seen flannel shirts, boots, hats, and such things, sold for a few knives or beads. What, in the name of Fortune, do these poor creatures want with trousers and shirts? I admit that if a man, knowing where he is going and what his work is to be, want some harmless article of European manufacture, there may be some excuse for letting him work for it; but I fail to see what excuse we can give for allowing ignorant captains and so called "Government agents," who know no word of the people's language, to go wherever they please and entice the natives on board their ships with red cloth or tobacco, and then carry them off to countries of which they know absolutely nothing. As to the much-talked-of three years' term, after which they are taken back to their homes, it is hardly necessary to point out that the natives have no more idea of what we mean by three years than a child in the nursery.

The whole labour trade system, therefore, I believe to be distinctly wrong as at present carried out, and very probably wrong however it were to be carried out, for we take the strongest men away from their homes at the best period of their lives, and as a rule we return them again demoralised and diseased; so that the whole social organisation of the native tribes is corrupted, and their numerical strength most alarmingly diminished.

The condition of the trade carried on in these seas in such articles as copra, bêche-de-mer, vegetable ivory, &c. &c., is no less unsatisfactory. There are no doubt some honest traders and respectable captains engaged in this business, but there are also, it must be confessed, some of the worst scoundrels in creation. These fellows, no less than the labour trade people, want careful watching, or their conduct is certain to produce trouble. Our men-of-war have hitherto spent a great deal too much time in the harbours of Sydney, Melbourne, and Hobart Town, and when they have gone down to the islands, it has, since Commodore Goodenough's time, been the custom merely to visit a few well-known places, and then return to some civilised settlement. There has indeed been practically no surveying done in this quarter of the Pacific for a long time, and to this day even the general bearings of a great part of many of the groups are not so much as approximately known. The charts are all antiquated and faultful, and I am certain that in very many places the French navigators of the last century were as well off in the matter of sailing directions as we are to-day.

It is satisfactory to know that Her Majesty's ships have been ordered to visit the islands more frequently than in the past, and to check as much as possible all acts of violence, whether committed by white man or black. This order was given none too soon, the cause of its issue being the news of a more serious massacre than any that has occurred since the attack upon Commodore Goodenough at Santa Cruz in 1875. The catastrophe to which I refer is the murder of Lieutenant-Commander Bower, of H.M. schooner *Sandfly*, and four seamen, who were killed in the Florida group in October 1880, without, apparently, the slightest provocation. The reason for this attack is in my judgment, however, simple enough. The natives have begun to disbelieve in the English war vessels; to quote the words of a native called Hailey,* chief of Coolangbangara, in the Solomon Islands—" White

---

* This man, in his message to Captain Ferguson announcing the Esperanza tragedy, from which a quotation is given above, introduces himself as follows—" The Hailey, king belong Coolangbangara, big feller fighting man; me speak you; me kiki (have eaten) ten one (eleven) feller man belong

man all same woman, he no savee fight, suppose women plenty cross she make plenty noise, suppose man-of-war he come fight me, he make plenty noise, but he all same woman—he no savee fight." This is their feeling. They see traders not unfrequently and labour ships pretty often, and they are told of the mighty vessels we possess which will destroy them all if they misbehave themselves. Many of them, however, have never seen these vessels at all, and at last believe the whole story to be a fabrication.

The murder of Lieutenant Bower is a terribly pertinent example of the state of things now existing in these seas. It happened, not at some place, like Santa Cruz, where white people are unknown, and the temerity of ignorance might be expected, but amongst islanders who were comparatively well informed concerning Englishmen and their power, but who at last had begun to discredit altogether what they had heard about our ability to administer punishment. I have in a previous chapter given a short account of the evening I spent at Gaeta. I was a night and part of two days, only a few weeks before the occurrence, in the very place from which these murderers came, and I do not hesitate to say that had this district

---

Esperanza ; me take him altogether trade—musket, powder, tobacco, bead, plenty ; me take everything ; me make big fire, ship he finish."

been visited once or twice in the year by a man-of-war, the natives would have been convinced by actual knowledge of what hitherto they had only learned from hearsay, and would not have dared therefore to have made such an attack upon a crew of white men.

The subsequent history of the *Sandfly* tragedy is one of great interest and importance. The culprits, after much trouble, were all captured, and with one exception, a boy of sixteen, executed; thus the power of our navy seems at last to have been thoroughly brought home to the inhabitants of the entire group. Of the manner in which all this was effected I have no space to write in this little volume; but the whole story may be found in the Blue Book lately published on the Natives of the Western Pacific and the Labour Traffic (C. 3641). One paragraph in the Commodore's despatch to the Lords of the Admiralty I am anxious to quote, on account of the graceful tribute paid to my friend Bishop Selwyn. It runs as follows:—

"I have much pleasure in calling my Lords' attention to the last paragraph on page 23 of Commander Bruce's despatch, where he speaks of the assistance, energy, and courage rendered and shown by the Right Reverend Bishop Selwyn, to whom mainly is due the credit of bringing the chiefs of Florida to reason, and inducing them to deliver up the murderers."

Before closing my observation upon Labour and Trade in the Western Pacific, I will ask those of my readers who care to form an opinion on this subject, to read through the following list of outrages which have occurred in the islands during the years 1875–1881 :—

January 1875.—The brig *James Birney* was taken by natives of an island in the Lord Howe's group. Captain Fletcher, together with eight white men and two coloured men, were killed.

August 1875.—The boats of H.M.S. *Pearl* were attacked at Nitendi, the main island of the Santa Cruz group ; Commodore Goodenough and two seamen were killed, three others were wounded.

July 1876.—The *Lucy and Adelaide* of Brisbane, labour vessel, was attacked at St. Bartholomew, an off-lying island of Espiritu Santo, New Hebrides. Captain Anderson was killed, and the boat's crew all wounded.

February 1877.—The schooner *Douglas* was attacked in the Louisiade archipelago. Two white men killed and five wounded.

November 1877.—A white trader named Easterbrook was murdered at Sulphur Bay, Tanna, New Hebrides.

1878.—The great rising in New Caledonia took place during this year, and over a hundred and fifty white people were killed. Since this occurrence the lives lost in desultory engagements between settlers and natives have been too numerous to mention.

May 1878.—A white trader was murdered at San Christoval, in the Solomon Islands.

June 1878.—A white trader named Morrow and one Savo boy were murdered near Marau Sound, Solomon Islands.

September 1878.—A boat's crew of the *May Queen* was cut out at Aragh, New Hebrides. The mate and a Tanna sailor were killed.

November 1878.—The schooner *Mystery* lost a boat and crew at Opa, New Hebrides. The Government agent and four natives were killed.

November 1878.—The *William Isler* of Cooktown was attacked at Brooker Island, Louisiade archipelago. A Mr. Ingram, white crew, two Chinamen, and three natives were killed.

As many as six parties of shipwrecked sailors are reported to have been murdered in this group.

November 1878.—James Martin, of the *Heather Bell*, was murdered at Opa, New Hebrides.

November 1878.—Robert Provis was murdered at Guadalcanar, Solomon Islands; also three natives.

December 1878.—Messrs. Irons and Arthur were murdered at Cloudy Bay, New Guinea.

May 1879.—Murder of Charlie at Marau Sound, Solomon Islands.

July 1879.—Murder of the mate and three of the

crew of schooner *Agnes Donald* at Aragh, New Hebrides.

August 1879.—Murder of Captain Levison by John Knowles at New Britain.

October 1879.—Murder of the mate of *Mavis* at the island of Tanna, New Hebrides.

October 1879.—Murder of crew of *Pride of Logan*, at Delele, New Guinea.

March 1880.—Murder of a white trader named Johnston at Opa, New Hebrides.

August 1880.—Murder of Fraser, the mate, and Nicholl, the Government agent, together with a boat's crew of the *Dauntless*, at Api, New Hebrides.

August 1880.—The auxiliary screw vessel *Ripple* was attacked at Bougainville, Solomon Islands. Captain Ferguson and five natives were killed; two white men seriously wounded.

September 1880.—The *Esparanza* attacked at New Georgia, Solomon Islands. Captain Mackintosh, the mate, a white sailor, and four natives were killed.

September 1880.—Murder of crew of Chinese junk at New Guinea.

October 1880.—The brigantine *Borealis* attacked at Ugi, Solomon Islands. Five white men and one Fijian were killed.

October 1880.—The cutter *Idalio* was attacked at Espiritu Santo, New Hebrides. Captain

McMillan and part of crew were killed. At the same time a boat was cut out, and all but two of its crew killed.

October 1880.—Murder of three white men, part of crew of *Loelia*, at Kabeira, New Britain.

October 1880.—Murder of crew of *Hongkong* at Leveade Island, New Britain.

October 1880.—Boat's crew of H.M.S. *Sandfly* attacked at Mandoliana, Floridas, Solomon Islands. Lieutenant-Commander Bower and four seamen killed.

November 1880.—Murder of Captain Foreman of the *Annie Brooks*, crew of eight white men, and three Chinamen, at Brooker Island, Louisiade archipelago.

November 1880.—The *Jabberwock* attacked at Tanna, New Hebrides; several lives lost.

November 1880.—Murder of nine Chinamen, being the crew of the *Prosperity*, in the Louisiade archipelago.

January 1881.—Schooner *Zephyr* attacked at Choiseul, Solomon Islands. Captain and crew murdered.

January 1881.—Murder of Captain Schwartz, of the *Leslie*, at Russell Island, Solomon Islands.

February 1881.—Murder of four Mission teachers at Kalo, New Guinea.

I may also mention the following outrages, of which I have not obtained full particulars:—The

Pearl and the *Marion Rennie* were both cut out at Rubiana, in the Solomon Islands. The *Dancing Wave* and the *Lavinia* were attacked and taken in the Floridas. Three whalers' boats' crews have been captured by the natives of the Treasury Islands, and four by those of the Lord Howe's group. A Captain Blake was recently killed at Simbo, near Rubiana, in the Solomon Islands, and a party of French naturalists were massacred at Basilisk Island in the autumn of 1880. Many other disasters have doubtless occurred in these seas during the last six years, but the above are those which have come more immediately under my notice.

As a corresponding subject for reflection I would ask my readers to notice this second list of island tragedies, contributed to the Melbourne *Argus* by Mr. Neilson, one of the oldest and most universally respected of South Sea Island missionaries. The following outrages are all the work of white men, and give a very fair idea of the kind of treatment the islanders are receiving from our countrymen in the South Seas. Mr. Neilson writes :—

" Allow me to give a few instances of the kind of things that are done in the islands.

" I knew a white man who employed some natives to work for him; in a fit of drunken recklessness he shot one of them dead. He underwent no trial, and received no punishment.

" I knew another white man who called out to

some natives who were in his employ to come and assist him quickly in something he was doing. He thought they were not coming quick enough, fired at them, and shattered the foot of one of them, so that he is a cripple for life. The white man was unpunished.

"I knew another white man who had a number of natives labouring under him, whom he used to follow in their work with a large whip, with which he flogged them when they were not giving him satisfaction. After a time this same man had bad sores on his feet, which prevented him from walking. He then got a litter made, on which he was carried round, and from which he flogged the natives.

"I knew a vessel in the labour trade that visited an island. The boat pulled in to the beach, and the sailors in her commenced dragging the women by force into the boat. The natives thereupon attacked the white sailors, killed them, and afterwards ate them. A ship of war went to punish the natives, who explained the state of matters to the captain. He exacted a fine of twenty-five pigs, and as this was not paid, he set fire to the natives' village and destroyed their property.

"I knew of a native on board of a ship who, for a trifling act of insubordination, was tied up to the mast and tortured to death, and no one was punished for it.

"I knew a white man who went ashore on an island, and said that he wanted to purchase a concubine, and offered a musket for one. A young man coveted the musket, dragged his own sister by force to the boat, and sold her into banishment. This white man and his concubine lived for a time close to me. Afterwards he left the island, but before doing so he sold his concubine to another white man for a case of gin.

"I knew another native woman who was taken by force as the concubine of a low white. At a game of cards she was gambled for, and won by another low white. The poor woman afterwards grew sick, and was not able to work for him, and he murdered her. The white man was not punished.

"The white man who began the labour traffic, and who was, I think, the greatest scoundrel I ever knew, told me that on a great many islands natives had destroyed their canoes, and went no more on sea voyages, as they were afraid of being kidnapped.

"I knew well a captain in the island trade who used to maintain that natives had no souls, and that it was no more harm to take their lives than to take the life of a dog. On two separate occasions I had considerable difficulty in dissuading captains of British ships of war from attacking natives who had been guilty of no crime but that of justifiable self-defence against the violence of white men. On both occasions I was happily successful.

"I knew a white man who in a fit of anger shot his native concubine dead. He pretended that his gun had gone off by accident, and was never even brought to trial.

"I knew of a party of eight natives who were taken to work on a plantation; they were so oppressed that at last they stole their master's boat and made their escape. On their way to their own island they were driven by stress of weather to another, where six of them were killed and eaten. The two others were rescued by a missionary at the risk of his own life.

"I knew of a party of eleven natives taken to Fiji, who were so ill-used by their master that they stole a boat and escaped, made their way to the New Hebrides, but did not reach their own island, and having fallen into the hands of heathens, one was killed, cooked, and eaten every evening until the whole were finished.

"I knew a white man who began a plantation and imported twenty-five natives to work it. He was unable to supply them properly with food, and before they could raise it for themselves, eight out of the twenty-five had perished from famine.

"I knew a white man who forcibly obtruded himself into a piece of land belonging to a native chief, and threatened that if the natives attempted to drive him away he would get a man-of-war to punish them. The natives, being alarmed at this threat, allowed him to remain.

"Attention having been directed to the character of the Government agents on the labour vessels, I have to state that I have seen a few of them, and knew pretty intimately two of them. One was a broken-down, unreformed drunkard. The captain of a ship-of-war said to me, 'I do not know what the Queensland Government mean by appointing a man like that. For a glass of whisky he would sign anything.' The other was a captain who had been engaged in the labour traffic, and who for irregularities had been removed from his command. He also was a drunkard, and a man who in addition was extremely reckless in the use of firearms. He was appointed Government agent in a Queensland vessel, and on his first voyage in that capacity he was wounded in the leg by a native spear. He died in consequence of his wound. On his deathbed he bitterly repented of his misdeeds, denounced the labour traffic as an abominable one, and wished that his life might be spared that he might expose its iniquities.

"I have known a considerable number of white men who have been killed by the natives while engaged in this trade, and while deploring their sad end, and regretting that they should have been cut down in the midst of their wickedness, I have in sober seriousness to express my decided conviction that most of them were men the cup of whose iniquity was full, and that they suffered the due reward of their deeds.

"Others, again, were men who had done no injury to the natives themselves, but upon whom the natives took revenge for the evil deeds of their countrymen; for the principle of national or tribal responsibility is held the whole world over by tribes and nations both savage and civilised.

"I beg, then, in conclusion, to call upon all Christian men, when they hear of massacres and outrages committed upon white men in the South Seas, not hastily to jump to the conclusion that the natives are invariably and chiefly to blame, and to state my firm conviction, as one having had perfect knowledge of this labour traffic from the very beginning, that ten natives have perished from the cruelty of the white man for every white man that has perished at the hands of the natives.

"I have abundance more of similar facts that are at your disposal should you wish for more. In the meantime allow me to subscribe myself—Yours, &c."

I do not think that any one, after reading the above pages, could seriously maintain that this question of Polynesian labour should be left only to time for solution ; it appears to me, indeed, to be one that cries aloud for investigation and reform.

We, who are the pioneers of civilisation in all corners of the globe, must surely be prepared to face the responsibilities of our mission as well as to reap the profit and the glory. For my own part, I look forward with the greatest hopes to the results of the Commission appointed by Government to inquire into the abuses in the labour trade. No one of late years has taken a wider or more highminded view of the native question in Polynesia than Sir Arthur Gordon, whose services upon the Commission have fortunately been secured, and I have therefore no doubt that the report which he and his colleagues are about to issue, will embody the wisest and most practical recommendations possible under the circumstances.

We shall then look to the Colonial Governments and to our own authorities to carry out these recommendations, and to organise an executive which will, in all honesty of purpose and energy of action, endeavour to suppress the abuses which have for so many years been a scandal in these seas.

The history of pioneering has truly been that of crime and abuse from the very earliest times, but we may hope in these latter days, being in possession of such infinite powers and marvellous resources, to minimise these evils, and so, bearing in mind the horrors of the Spanish aggression in the West, and of our own and other nations' cruelties practised amongst a thousand wild races, do our very uttermost to leave behind us a fair name and history as the inheritance of a future generation of colonists in these sunny lands of the WESTERN PACIFIC.

THE END.

LONDON : PRINTED BY WILLIAM CLOWES AND SONS, LIMITED, STAMFORD STREET AND CHARING CROSS.

BY

WALTER COOTE, F.R.G.S.

New and Cheaper Edition, Crown 8vo. 10s. 6d.

This Work is beautifully illustrated by forty-seven original Engravings, executed under the direction of EDWARD WHYMPER *from Sketches by the* AUTHOR, *Native Drawings, &c. The volume, which is furnished with a large Track Chart of the World, and also a Chart of the Western Pacific, contains an account of the Author's travels during a period of four years, and is divided into parts, in the following way:—*

PART I.—Queensland; New South Wales and Victoria: New Zealand; Norfolk Island, and the Fiji Islands.

PART II.—The Sandwich Islands, including a Visit to the Great Volcano of Kilauea; The New Hebrides, Banks', Torres, Solomon, and Loyalty Islands; A Visit to the fatal Santa Cruz Group, and a description, with many illustrations, of the Natives of those Islands; An Account of the French Colony of New Caledonia, and a General Summary of Missionary Work in Polynesia, and the Condition of Labour and Trade.

PART III.—The China Ports; Foochow, and the Tea Districts; The Nagasendo Road through the heart of Japan; Nikko, Tokio, and Kioto.

PART IV.—Central America; Lima, and the Great Andes Railroad; Santiago and Southern Chile; La Plata and Brazil.

LONDON:
SAMPSON LOW, MARSTON, SEARLE, & RIVINGTON,
CROWN BUILDINGS, 188, FLEET STREET, F.C.

SOME OPINIONS OF THE PRESS.

THE SPECTATOR.—
"The work of an intelligent and candid observer."

THE SATURDAY REVIEW.—
"We have read it with a good deal of pleasure. Mr. Coote has an intelligent mind and an attentive eye. . . . . We should have liked to touch on other portions of our author's narrative; but we have, we trust, said enough to lead our readers themselves to accompany him in his 'Wanderings South and East.'"

THE ATHENÆUM.—
"The author hits off in a lively, humorous way the characteristic features of the towns and landscapes of the South American sea-board. He shows both vigour and shrewdness too in his notes of a flying visit to China and Japan. The book-buyer will feel indebted to the author for the reproduction of some Japanese drawings of extraordinary cleverness, and, indeed, all the illustrations are good."

THE ACADEMY.—
"The author sees and thinks for himself; with a few lively touches he brings scenes and places vividly before us, and we can heartily recommend his fresh and pleasant book."

PALL MALL GAZETTE.—
"Mr. Coote does not say whether his object was to travel or to make a book, but it very soon becomes evident that he is, at all events, able to write. His style is not much like the ordinary traveller's, being terse, and straightforward. . . . It is a very interesting book, and it is furnished with capital maps and a number of lively illustrations."

NONCONFORMIST.—
"Mr. Coote's book is both sensible and entertaining. . . . it is fully up to the mark of interest, which will make good his claim to be read and pondered. We cannot follow this happy and observant traveller to other islands; but we have said enough to induce our readers to accept such pleasant companionship, and to look at these interesting lands by the help of Mr. Coote's graphic and facile pen."

CHRISTIAN WORLD.—
"We very warmly commend this handsome volume to our readers."

Opinions of the Press—*continued.*

BRITISH QUARTERLY REVIEW.—
"The book is readable and interesting, and in some of its chapters really presents substantive additions to our stock of facts. . . . It is in every respect a very beautiful book."

THE GUARDIAN.—
"There is much food for reflection in Mr. Coote's narratives and descriptions."

LAND AND WATER.—
"We do not remember to have read a narrative of varied travel which interests the reader so entirely from beginning to end. The book is illustrated by nearly fifty engravings and two excellent maps. Altogether Mr. Coote's 'Wanderings' is sure to give unfailing pleasure both to the travelled and untravelled reader."

THE FIELD.—
"The Loyalty Islands, New Caledonia, New Hebrides, Santa Cruz, and Solomon Islands were all visited in turn. Mr. Coote's record will doubtless be perused with the greatest interest. All this part of the book is too good to extract or condense; it must be read. . . . We can cordially recommend the volume to our readers."

THE DAILY TELEGRAPH.—
"Mr. Coote is a shrewd observer, writes well, and as the work is accompanied by some very good sketches, it is doubly valuable."

THE STANDARD.—
"Mr. Coote is evidently an able and practised writer. . . . His work is one that will be extensively read and generally liked."

LITERARY WORLD.—
"Mr. Coote is to be highly complimented upon his excellent success in the narratives of his manifold experiences."

JOURNAL OF THE ROYAL GEOGRAPHICAL SOCIETY.—
"This book contains a very interesting narrative referring to the New Hebrides, Basuto, Torres, Santa Cruz, Solomon, and Loyalty Islands, which were visited by the author in company with Bishop Selwyn under peculiar circumstances, this party being the first to land on some of the most dangerous islands since the punishment inflicted in 1875 for the murder of Commodore Goodenough. . . . . The author's observations on the natives generally, with the excellent illustrations, will be found of considerable interest."

Opinions of the Press.—*continued.*

Harper's Monthly Magazine.—

"We have seldom met with a book so free from the usual defects of this class of literature; the narrative goes on in an easy and natural manner, the descriptions being all the writer's own—the information honestly obtained through his own keenly observant faculties. . . . Mr. Coote has enriched his volume with maps and illustrations, which are of great service to the reader."

The Graphic.—

"Mr. Coote's style is entirely readable, and unlike most of his brethren in this class of literature, he writes good English."

The Illustrated London News.—

"An entertaining volume. . . . There is a multitude of engravings, besides two charts of the ocean voyages, to illustrate these four years' wanderings."

The Melbourne Argus.—

"Mr. Coote has produced a well-condensed and pleasantly-written descriptive record."

The Daily News.—

"A narrative which has a welcome freshness both of style and matter, arising in great part from the active curiosity and unfailing interest which the writer displays in all that is characteristic and significant. Mr. Coote is an intelligent commentator on national characteristics and national tendencies, and often suggests a view which commends itself to the reader's judgment both for novelty and truth."

Nature.—

"Mr. Coote is a good observer, and the information he gives concerning what he saw in the less frequented islands, the New Hebrides, the Santa Cruz, Solomon, and Loyalty Islands, is a welcome addition to existing knowledge. The illustrations are good, and the volume as a whole is extremely pleasant reading."

www.ingramcontent.com/pod-product-compliance
Lightning Source LLC
Chambersburg PA
CBHW020916230426
43666CB00008B/1466